Ending the Global Casino?

ENDING THE GLOBAL CASINO?

AD BROERE

HUMANE ECONOMY PUBLISHINGS, DECEMBER 2010

Copyright © 2010   by Humane Economy Publishings, The Netherlands
Website: www.endingtheglobalcasino.org
Author: Ad Broere
Cartoons: Jos Collignon, Karl Wimer
Editing: Marja Anderton Ph.D., Michelle Ledford
Process coach: Michelle Ledford
Cover design/layout: Peter Beemsterboer
ISBN: 978-90-816280-1-3

Printed in U.K. by Lightning Source, London
Distribution: Lightning Source
First edition: December 2010

CONTENTS

Acknowledgements

*I thank Anneke for her patience, and
for the support she has given me
during the writing process. Her
answers on my questions helped me a
lot to make the right choices.*

*Thank you Michelle for your
constant belief in my ability to write
my second book in English. You have
encouraged me to go on when there
were the inevitable dips, and you gave
me your honest, always useful
feedback, each time I did send you
evidence of the work in progress.*

*Marja, thanks to you the quality
of the written English is on the level
the reader may expect from a book
with a message intended to be taken
seriously.*

*Further, I thank Jos Collignon
and Karl Wimer for their brilliant
cartoons, and Peter Beemsterboer
for his excellent cover design.*

Foreword

The world's financial systems are shaking. At this moment, autumn 2010, the focus is on the euro. That does not mean that the dollar, yen, sterling and other currencies are not under pressure. It appears that the attention is being distracted from those other currencies in a many fold action that looks like a deliberate attempt to destroy the euro. It seems that those who have considered this have been rather successful up till now. In spite of the 1 trillion euro support given by the European Central Bank and the IMF to sustain the weak countries such as Greece, there is evidently a deep lack of confidence in the future of the Euro.

The economy of Greece and the Greek people are at the edge of total disaster. Attempts to re-arrange the economic structure are not successful. If the enormous debts Greece have are written off a wave of problems will come over the financial world, especially the Northern European countries and banks. They are deeply involved in the problems of the so-called PIIGS countries (Portugal, Italy, Ireland, Greece, and Spain). At the same time there are the problems between China and the U.S.. China is the biggest creditor of the U.S. The debt of the U.S. is immense, a total of many trillions of dollars. It is the consequence of decades of purchases of U.S. treasury paper to support the financial position of that country, keeping the dollar high against the Chinese currency (yuan) and thus sustaining the massive Chinese exports to the U.S. Yet, the emerging markets are flooded with out of thin air created dollars, now that the economies of the rich western countries appear to be unable to find the way up again, and dollars can be borrowed at low interest rates. The ever growing money supply of the U.S. has increased China's fear of the downfall of the dollar. Because of this China is trying to reduce their dollar balance. One of the methods to realise reduction is to decrease the trade in dollars. Therefore it is not in China's interest for the eurozone to be in big trouble. Also Japan and the U.K. play a role in the 'game'. Both countries struggle with high government debts, and failing exports.

Where it all will end is hard to predict, but somewhere and somehow it will happen. The financial and political instability worldwide and the lack of international consensus are the main reasons that it will go wrong. And possibly – sooner than we think – as we don't really want to be hoping for the downfall.

In the mean time speculators go on with their activities. Big private investors, hedge funds, investment banks keep on gambling on anything. As long as it brings cash returns it is all right. It is clear that they contribute to a great extent to the instability of the financial system. Trade in gold and silver is booming. People try to save their capital by investing in those precious metals. The demand for gold and silver is much higher than the supply, leading to ever increasing prices. More institutions and analysts are warning of a collapse. In a report issued by McKinsey in February 2010 titled 'Debt and Deleveraging' this institute concludes that the 'Argentine scenario' is the most probable one. This means that the artificially low inflation policy of the central

banks will fail, hyperinflation will follow, and as in Argentina all of a sudden the value of currencies will drop to virtually zero. This is the biggest fear of all governments, all over the world. Because it will lead to massive uprisings, protests, instability, and more major problems.

What might be the consequence of this? I think it is in the mind of the – in this book referred to as – new world order planners. In my opinion what is unfolding now on the world stage has been foreseen by people in powerful positions. They have designed strategies on what to do after the total collapse of the present financial economic system. Most probable is the issuance of a new world currency. Ordinary people all over the world may pay the price for this, by losing most of their properties, because the majority of private households have gone deeply in debt in order to finance their homes and other purchases they could not afford to pay out of their savings. It speaks for itself that this radical change will not go without upheavels. It is therefore reasonable to think that the planners will use control and restriction of freedom as instruments to introduce the new world order smoothly. Probably they will eliminate negative elements that obstruct the development of a world of peace and prosperity. Who the negative elements are is of course 'in the eye of the beholder'.

Whatever will come it will not be a democracy, where people have real liberty. If a new system reigns, it will be led by 'a few' as it is impossible to allow people themselves to decide about their own lives, because such a system will be based on rules, laws and control. A completely different scenario would be a world where people are willing to cooperate without selfishness and greed and directed to a sustainable world that they can leave happily to their children. An economy wherein wealth is also measured by the extent of happiness and health might develop. No control, no rules, nor propaganda. This would be a future to dream of. However, reality is different. Unlimited greed, unrealistically high bonuses, making money with money, it all goes on. And it would be an illusion to think that things would suddenly change through a collapse. Of course there are people who are striving for a better world. Unfortunately they are too scattered and act too much on a stand-alone basis. It would be great though, if we collectively would not have to go through the bitter experience of a centrally led financial economic system. Hopefully this book will contribute to the radical change in mindset necessary to make us free from compulsion and lack of freedom.

In this book I do not want to point an accusing finger at individual people as the ones who cause all the misery we are in now. It would be too easy to say he or she or they are bad, whatever that is. The following quote is very appropriate in this context:

> 'The dividing line between good and evil goes right through the heart of the human being' — ALEKANDR SOLSJENITZIN

The Treaty of Lisbon, designed to make the EU better manageable, and initially rejected by the Irish in 2008, was in 2009 accepted after a number of mainly financial concessions by the EU to Ireland.

Are you ready to lose everything? Even your freedom? Well, then let things happen! But if you do not want the misery to come over you, wake up and do something. This book can help you to make up your mind.

Ad Broere

CHAPTER 1

What caused the Financial crisis?

'Money is the root of all evil' is an ancient, biblical expression which is even commonly used nowadays, for instance in song-texts. Greed is one of the basic instincts that makes finance and economy work the way it does. Unlimited greed and the pursuit for ever more possessions is what it appears to be all about in life and this leads to the extremes that happen in the financial world. It has already lead to several major crisis, in the 20th (for examples the great depression in the 1930s) and the 21st centuries and as there has been no change in attitude since, and we can only wait for more disaster to come.

The 'haute finance' has dominated the financial world over the last decades. The Wall Street wizards developed a multitude of financial 'products' that have altered financial institutes into true casinos. These financial products are derivatives of the financial value of tangible products such as raw materials, real estate, etc. The world the traders of derivatives live in is far from reality. No wonder that many of them live unrealistic lives.

Adjiedj Bakas, author of 'Beyond the crisis', links the widespread use of cocaine to the hectic culture in the main financial centers. Addressing six hundred bankers on a Financial Forum, he said 'one of the big disadvantages of cocaine is that the user completely loses any sense of proportion. This is one of the main reasons that the many traders addicted to the drug would not stop where they should have.

The magnitude of trade in derivatives is that overwhelming that the sum of all transactions is more than ten times bigger as the value of all what the whole world produces. Two examples illustrate the trade in derivatives.

Firstly, a U.S. Bank has issued mortgages at a value of $1 billion.For this amount this bank cashes yearly $100 million interest from the lenders. The bank gets signals that a growing number of mortgage clients have difficulties in keeping up with their payments. The bank wants to get rid of this risk, and sells the complete package of mortgages to an investment bank at a 10% discount. Consequently the investment bank cuts the package in three parts. One with a small risk on nonpayment, the second with what you might call a medium risk, and the third part with a big risk of nonpayment. The part that carries the least risk will probably be paid back fully. The amount of this segment is $ 400 million. It is named 'Senior'. The second part called Mezzanine and is riskier. The qualification for this part is medium risk. This segment involves $300 million. The third part is very risky. The potential loss in this segment is very big and is named Equity. It too involves $300 million.

Now the Collaterised Debt Obligations (CDOs) come on the scene. A CDO is an example of a derivative financial product. This financial product is collateralised because there are assets to secure the debt. It is an obligation, because the investment bank sells the financial product to other financial institutes, pension funds, insurance companies etc.

The investment bank sells three types of CDOs:
- Senior CDOs at a low risk and thus a relatively low return of 5%.
- Mezzanine CDOs at a medium risk, and a return of 7%
- Equity CDOs carrying a big risk on nonpayment and a big return of 14%.

The investment bank pays yearly $ 83 million to its CDO investors, and has a return of $ 100 million on the mortgages they had purchased. The balance is a positive $ 17 million each year. That is, as long as all goes well. Good enough to pay attractive bonuses to their top managers. The investment bank has a good reputation. Therefore, institutes such as Moody's, and Standard & Poor's are willing to qualify the bank for a triple A status, which according to these institutes is as solid as a rock. In their purchasing policies virtually all financial institutes have a blind faith in the qualifications of Moody's, and Standard & Poor's.

As 75% of the financial institutes still had a triple A qualification in 2007 you can imagine what happened. The art of investing is to have an 'as high as possible return' at an 'as low as possible risk'. Pension funds, life insurance companies etc. were all very keen on the CDOs. The investment bank in this example did not have any difficulty in selling the CDOs. The full $1 billion dollars were cashed, and the initial profit of $ 100 million as the difference between buying the mortgages and selling the CDOs was made.

Consequently the nonpayment problems started. An increasing number of mortgage lenders defaulted. But as the investment bank got rid of the risk by selling the CDO's the real losers were the buyers of them and not the investment bank. In the end the problem was mainly caused by the mortgage bankers that granted mortgage loans to people who were not able by far to repay their debts. And as we all know now, this has happened in the United States. Fanny May and Fanny Mac, two huge mortgage banks sold loans to people that could barely afford the debt. Television programs showed the seemingly endless number of empty houses, left by those who were hit by foreclosure. By selling the CDO's the financial problem was exported all over the world. Of course not just institutes such as the investment bank were to blame. Also the buyers all over the world that went blind on the triple A qualification and did not even bother to do their own risk evaluation were wrong.

The second example of the fruits of 'haute finance' are the Credit Default Swaps (CDS). Pension Fund Decent is not allowed to grant loans to companies with a lower than a double A status, therefore, automotive company Rush does not fulfill this demand. However, Rush is very keen on a $ 1 billion loan from Decent, they are even prepared to pay 10% interest on the loan. Nevertheless, no chance! However, there is a helping hand. Insurance Company Assistance is prepared to intermediate between Decent and Rush. At a premium of 1% per year Assistance assures Decent to cover the damage should Rush go bankrupt.

And as the loan qualification institutes mentioned earlier have given Assistance a double A status, Rush can have the desired loan from Decent. Pension Fund Decent grants the loan, receives $ 100 million per year interest from Rush and pays $ 10 million premium per year to Assistance. Thus, a net return of 9% on an investment of $ 1 billion. That is indeed very satisfying for a risk avoiding institute!

Likewise Assistance has 1,000 similar contracts. The total risk run by Assistance is $ 1000 billion. In order to have full coverage for this amount the cash position of Assistance would have to be immense. Of course this is not attainable. Assistance has no more than a fraction available in case of bankruptcies.

Assurance company Risky is just like Assistance involved in the fate of Rush. A hedge fund has negotiated a Credit Default Swap with Risky. The bet is that Risky pays out $ 1 billion if Rush goes bankrupt within three years from now. Risky receives $ 20 million premium on a yearly basis from the hedge fund. Other than Assistance is this Credit Default Swap is purely based on betting. Hedge Funds use a multitude of financial instruments such as derivatives to achieve a positive return under all circumstances. Therefore Hedge Funds are very popular with the big investors and the extremely rich. Even during times of down going markets hedge funds manage to make good returns for their clients.

Automotive company Rush goes bankrupt after two years. Both Insurance companies Assistance and Risky pay out $ 1 billion. Insurance company Assistance has enough solvency to survive this blow. Risky however is downgraded because their financial position has become unstable. Pension Fund Decent will have no problem. Other pension funds however did have contracts with Risky. They have no other choice then but to end the loan contracts that came into being as between Rush and Decent. This of course causes a lot of trouble. It is easy to imagine what will happen if there are a series of bankruptcies. And it is also clear why the American government could not afford General

Motors to go bankrupt. Because of the vast figures involved, Credit Default Swaps are a major sword over the head of the financial system.

These two examples are just a small part of many more of how the 'haute finance' earned a lot in the golden years and at the same time caused a lot of potential trouble. Because although most of the investment bankers and hedge funds did make a lot of money, they exported the trouble at the same time. In the end someone has always to pay the bill.

An example: In 2007 41% of all the value in goods and services produced in the U.S. was for the account of the financial industry. No wonder that this betting circus that went far beyond the underlying real values had to go wrong. And this did happen end of the year 2007. People that could not pay the interest on their mortgages and businesses that had cash problems that caused the big balloon to explode. And instead of a complete renovation governments have chosen to patch up the financial system. A mega injection of taxpayers' money has kept the system upright for the time being. But nothing has changed whatsoever since. The same attitude that has caused the financial crisis is still the driving force behind it all.

It would be easy to isolate evil somewhere outside of us. Then we might be able to get rid of it once and for all, however, reality is much more complex. Therefore it may be wise to get a better insight into both the financial and the economic system. How do they work and how does the one influence the other? How is everything interrelated and that what consequences does what happens in one part of the system for the other parts?

Being fully aware of our complete dependency on each other, more and more people might be prepared to make the necessary changes in their lives. I will not be unrealistically optimistic about this, though. Some people are that greedy, selfish, and hungry for more money and more

power that it appears they are unable to change their ways as long as the present monetary system exists. The American journalist Matt Taibi wrote a shocking article about the role of Goldman Sachs: The Great American Bubble Machine. The first lines of the article are as follows:

> From tech stocks to high gas prices, Goldman Sachs has engineered every major market manipulation since the Great Depression — and they're about to do it again. The first thing you need to know about Goldman Sachs is that it's everywhere. The world's most powerful investment bank is a great vampire squid wrapped around the face of humanity, relentlessly jamming its blood funnel into anything that smells like money. In fact, the history of the recent financial crisis, which doubles as a history of the rapid decline and fall of the suddenly swindled dry American empire, reads like a Who's Who of Goldman Sachs graduates.

SOURCE: HTTP://WWW.ROLLINGSTONE.COM/POLITICS/NEWS/ , 5 APRIL 2010, THE GREAT AMERICAN BUBBLE MACHINE

To make the right decisions it is necessary to be informed. Therefore it is useful to get a better insight into both the monetary and the economic system. How do they work and how does the one influence the other? How is everything interrelated, and what consequences does what happens in one part of the system for the other parts? I will answer these questions in the next Chapters.

CHAPTER 2

Economy

'The richest one percent of this country owns half our country's wealth, five trillion dollars. One third of that comes from hard work, two thirds comes from inheritance, interest on interest accumulating to widows and idiot sons and what I do, stock and real estate speculation. It's bullshit. You got ninety percent of the American public out there with little or no net worth. I create nothing. I own. We make the rules, pal. The news, war, peace, famine, upheaval, the price per paper clip. We pick that rabbit out of the hat while everybody sits out there wondering how the hell we did it. Now you're not naive enough to think we're living in a democracy, are you buddy? It's the free market. And you're a part of it. You've got that killer instinct. Stick around pal, I've still got a lot to teach you'.

GORDON GEKKO IN OLIVER STONE'S MOVIE *WALL STREET*

The axiom the economic science is built on is that man has unlimited material needs and scarce resources to satisfy them. Furthermore, rational choices are made on what to buy with the available resources (money). True to this axiom economists have placed the consumer in a central role. The consumer is not king, he is the goal of all efforts to make him buy whatever companies want to sell. Marketing has been developed to support companies to achieve this goal. Marketers are true psychologists. They know what makes the consumer tick. Of course, the marketing instrument is primarily available for the big companies, foremost multinationals. This already causes a shift between larger and smaller companies. The grip that large companies have on the market is to great extent due to successful marketing. The success of marketing also proves that people are predictable in their buying patterns.

Another consequence of the economists' vision on man is, that companies aim to earn as much as possible in the short term. The needs of the shareholders of these companies are unlimited, aren't they? And to fulfill those needs there is a continuous demand for more money. Shareholder value is the main goal for the majority of companies. Shareholder value is in fact the amount of money available for shareholders, earned by any company. Obviously, the more the better.

Companies pay out dividends to their shareholders if enough profit has been made. Nevertheless dividends are not the main goal of many investors, because they speculate on holding gain. Holding gain is the positive difference between the buying and selling price of a share. There are share investors that make marginal holding gains per share in a very short time. Still the total profit may be big because of the large volume of shares they buy and sell. Also there are investors who do not even buy or sell shares but just the right to buy or sell shares. Call options are the right to buy shares, and put options the right to sell. Having an option means that you do not need to have the shares themselves. The trade in options is mainly for speculative reasons.
It is clear that the trade in shares as described above is not even remotely related to an involvement with the company itself. The company is mainly considered a cash machine or cash cow. As long as the machine works it is all right. What makes the machine work is of a lesser interest. Students at business schools soon learn to understand this. When they produce a business plan in the context of their education, they learn that the ultimate goal is to maximise profits whatever business they set up. Sustainability and social corporate responsibility are fashionable and good for the company's image but not to be taken too seriously.

In large companies, management is separated from ownership. Management has the responsibility to achieve the goals set and approved by the general meeting of shareholders, which is theoretically the highest decision maker in rank, because, in the end it are the shareholders who own the company. Nevertheless because of the millions of small shareholders, top management in large companies often apply the divide and rule principle successfully. This has been certainly true in the past. Nowadays, however, there are the so-called activist investor groups that put pressure on the management of any company they have a stake in to act in accordance with their demands.

If shareholders choose short term return, management has to perform accordingly. They receive high financial rewards if goals are met, and if not they may have to look for other jobs. No wonder that management is and has always been keen on cutting costs. A proven approach is to produce goods in low wage countries.

Local governments in Asia for instance, have helped multinational enterprises over the last decades to produce at low expense at the cost of the traditional culture, the socio- economic structure and environment. Countries with a stable economy based on agriculture have been disintegrated through the influence of the multinationals. Lots of people in rural areas have become unemployed and have had to move to the cities hoping they could find work. If they did so the money they earned would have been barely enough for a decent living. There have also been vast numbers of people that have remained unemployed. Child labour, criminality and prostitution have flourished in those areas.

If the management of any big company should fail, they may lose the trust of their shareholders. If the value of the shares drop there is the danger that equity funds or investment bankers take over the complete company. Often these funds have already a stake in many of the big corporations. If the management fails there is the option of taking over all the shares, if not in a friendly takeover bid than in a hostile one. Equity investors are always keen on good opportunities. What happens after such a takeover is often bad for many of the employees. The new masters' goal is primarily to protect their own return on investment, disregarding the interests of the employees. For example the British equity investor Lion Capital that took over the Dutch retail organization Hema in 2007. After three years of cutting expenses and destroying the business culture by forcing the human capital over the edge, Lion Capital wants in 2010 to sell Hema. Of course with the firm intent to make a big profit. (Source: HP/de Tijd 10 September 2010, 'De teloorgang van het Hema-gevoel')

Another example of a very powerful private equity firm is The Carlyle Group:

The Carlyle Group is a global private equity investment firm, based in Washington, D.C. with more than $84.5 billion of equity capital under management, diversified over 64 different funds as of March 31, 2009. The firm operates four fund families, focusing on leveraged buyouts, growth capital, real estate and leveraged finance investments. The firm employs more than 890 employees, including 495 investment professionals in 20 countries with several offices in the Americas, Europe, Asia, and Australia its portfolio companies employ more than 415,000 people worldwide. Carlyle has over 1300 investors in 71 countries. Carlyle was ranked in 2008 as the largest private equity firm in the world, according to a ranking called the PEI 50 based on capital under management. Second place in the ranking is Goldman Sachs Principal Investment Area.

An example of Carlyle's recent activities; Global alternative asset manager The Carlyle Group announced on 3 August 2010 the first closing of its RMB Fund, which is now ready to invest. The RMB Fund, which has a target size of RMB 5 billion (approximately US$740 million), will make investments in large growth companies in Beijing and across China. Carlyle has received more than RMB2.4 billion (approximately US$350 million) in commitments from a variety of sources, including: Beijing State-owned Capital Operation and Management Center (BSCOMC), Beijing Equity Investment Development Fund, as well as other large SOEs, private companies and individuals.

SOURCE: WIKIPEDIA

The existence of equity funds stimulates management to give priority to shareholder value.

Recent research by Dr. P.J. Bezemer has pointed out that nearly three quarters of all big companies give priority to shareholder value. Shares of the remaining quarter of companies are mainly in the hands of families, and for the majority of them the primary goal is the wealth of the family. Shareholder value appears to be contradictory to long term investments. That is why big companies often are reluctant to try something completely new, like switching to an environmentally friendly and sustainable production. This might lower profitability for a number of years. And that will not be appreciated by the shareholders. The conclusion therefore is, that the majority of multinational companies are being held in a firm grip by their shareholders.

Big fossil energy companies such as Exxon and Shell go clearly for shareholder value. They do not like adventures. The level of investment in the development of environmentally friendly energy is marginal compared to their total turnover, and their overall investments. They strictly cling to oil and gas. This issue will be discussed more in-depth in Chapter 3.

In 2007, three years before the oil disaster in the Gulf of Mexico, BP tried to convince people of their involvement with durable energy.

We estimate that if 10% of the world's power came from wind, it would cut CO2 emissions by one billion tonnes per year
The challenge for BP is expanding its wind operations to form a material business – that means owning and operating gigawatts of installed power.

BP is developing wind farm projects in key markets
We are developing projects in the US, India and China for onshore operations and North West Europe for offshore operations. In doing

so we are using technology to select the best wind turbines and ensure a consistent and secure supply of energy.

Maximizing commercial advantage
To achieve commercial advantage from wind farm operations, BP works with specialist companies to collect data on wind speed, direction, temperature and pressure, while also pursuing advances in meteorological modeling from academia.

BP invests in ensuring it has ready access to advances in wind turbine technology, which is evolving constantly and rapidly.

Advancing wind technology
To support its wind operations, BP is exploring engineering and design issues in partnership with the University of Manchester, UK. We are also exploring advances in offshore turbines with technology development partners in the UK Energy Technologies Institute, and drawing on the expertise of electrical engineers at China's Tsinghua University to apply western wind models to China's landscape and market.

Exceeding all growth projections
In the context of a growing market worldwide, BP's wind business has grown tenfold in two years. We have invested $825 million in wind since the launch of the Alternative Energy business in 2005, with a further $600 million planned for 2008. BP expects its wind business to have commissioned 1,000 megawatts by the end of 2008 and to grow at more than 80% per year between now and 2010, well in excess of the market.

SOURCE: WWW.BP.COM 2008

Shorter than a year after the above mentioned statements of BP on their own website the media announced a change in strategy:

> The British Oil Company BP will invest a considerable lower amount
> in alternative energy sources, such as bio fuels, solar- and wind en-
> ergy. BP plans to increase the production of oil and gas.
>
> SOURCE: HET FINANCIEELE DAGBLAD 3 MARCH 2009

As stated above the majority of shareholders is primary interested in profit through buying and selling shares. This focus on the short term contributes to a conservative attitude towards major innovative investments. This is bad for the long term health of private enterprise. No wonder that people who are concerned about this make an appeal to investors to act differently.

For example: Hans Wijers, CEO of the Dutch multinational corporation Akzo. In an interview he stated that ways should be explored to reward loyal shareholders better, both in financial terms, and for their degree of participation in the business. According to Wijers, 'unfriendly speculators determine a company's agenda. It is very hard to deal with this group of shareholders because their goals divert from those of the company' He is not the only top manager who has pointed out the dangers for the future of private enterprise. Yet no substantial changes have been made until now.

This is one of the main reasons why extremes such as the following example keep on recurring: The British baby clothing retail chain Mothercare purchased clothing from an Indian supplier that used workers work for 48 hours per week at a wage of less than 10 rupiahs (18 eurocents) per hour. Mothercare was confronted with this abuse by the British newspaper The Guardian. They had to respond swiftly and properly in order to minimise the damage to their image, by asserting their clientele that suppliers like these are not welcome. According to Mothercare they had not allowed this Indian supplier if only they had been aware....

According to the Indian activist Swamin Agnivesh this is only a small glimpse of what is actually happening. His calculations show that 65 million Indians lead a life of slavery, for example, workers in the metro in Delhi who have long working days under ground without access to drinking water and toilets. Perhaps the most extreme and devastating phenomenon is the existence of so-called bonded labourers. Workers who have received an advance amount that they are never able to pay back, due to usury interest. Often these debts are passed on from father to son.

I have explained why multinationals are generally tied to their shareholders but what about the small and medium sized companies (SMEs)? If they have shareholders they are in a different position. Often shareholders of the smaller companies are completely involved with the business itself. So, one could expect a different attitude. Nevertheless reality is that many small and medium sized companies are to a great extent dependent on big companies. This is because SMEs often deliver products and services to the big companies. Examples of these companies are transporting, engineering and maintenance, and security services companies plus producers of home brand products in the food retail industry. In the end it is all about the favour of the consumer.

The importance of the consumer is proven by the role of the so-called Consumer Confidence Index as a vital indicator for the health of the economy. Man in his role as consumer in general clearly complies with the economic axiom. He has unlimited needs and scarce resources. Therefore companies offer their products and services at the lowest possible price. I will return to this subject in the chapter Consumerism.

If the wage level in a country becomes too high, multinationals seek areas where cheap labour is available. China's leading position in clothing manufacturing, for example, is underlined by the fact, that 53% of wool used in manufacturing by the top-ten producing countries, and 45% of cotton is consumed by China. India is second with 12% of wool, and 19% of cotton consumption in clothing production. Because of the large production volumes, China is also a major importer; wool from New Zealand and Australia, and cotton from India and – notably – the United States, which is a net exporter of cotton. There are more industries in which China has a major position. This explains why China is keen on safeguarding the supply of commodities such as copper, lead, zinc, nickel, and rubber. The need for aluminium, and coal can – for the time being – be covered by domestic production. Yet, an increasing consciousness of the bad influence of coal on the environment makes that China is in a transition process to other energy sources, such as natural gas and oil. The United States is by far the biggest consumer of oil and natural gas, and a major net importer. This sets the stage for the competition for energy resources in the near future. The top proved oil reserves in percentages end 2009 were: Saudi Arabia 19.8%, Venezuela 12.9%, Iran 10.3%, Iraq 8.6%, Kuwait 7.6%, United Arab Emirates 7.3%, Russia 5.6%, and Libya 3.3%. The conclusion is justified that as long as the major economic powers base the energy consumption on oil and gas, there will be a special interest for the countries mentioned above.... (source: The Economist Pocket World in Figures 2011 edition)

Also over the past decades more and more companies have switched from a labour driven to an automation driven production process. Examples of this development can be found amongst many others in the automotive industry, storage and transport of containers in big harbours, and food processing. Automation in itself is not a bad thing. Monotonous labour has been replaced by machines. However, many of the former workers did not benefit from this improvement. Automation of the production primarily served shareholders value.

It is said that countries such as the U.K., Germany, and The Netherlands have developed a service economy after the production automation wave and the shift of labour to low wage countries. Trade, transport, and high level technology are said to be the strong aspects of this economy. However, countries that rely deeply on services become in the end completely dependent on the product producing countries. Countries? Or should we say multinationals that control production anywhere. If services are not needed anymore because these can also be performed better, cheaper, and based on a solid knowledge base, as for example by upcoming nations like India, in the end there will be a lot of unemployment and poverty in the countries once economically powerful.

Multinational companies do not demonstrate any social responsibility towards their own employees, let alone the population of any country. Therefore, the only cure for countries such as U.K., Germany, The Netherlands, etc. will be by giving plenty of room to the small- and medium sized businesses especially those that develop durable products, renewable energy forms, and care for the environment and humanity. Luckily there are more and more people who are willing to work for the renovation of the economy.

The biggest problem SMEs meet is financially funding the business. Banks and private investors are not very keen on small- and medium sized businesses. Generally financial institutes consider SMEs as too risky. Especially those that want to start something completely new. Therefore I will focus on the financial world and its monetary system in Chapters 4 and 5.

CHAPTER 3

Fossils and renewable energy

OIL COMPANIES AND SHAREHOLDER VALUE

The five big western oil and gas corporations Exxon-Mobil, Royal Dutch-Shell, British Petroleum-Amoco, Chevron-Texaco and Total made huge profits in the years 2004-2006.

This table shows the net profits (after tax):

(x million $)	Exxon	Shell	BP	Texaco	Total
2004	25,330	19,257	17,262	13,328	11,149
2005	36,130	26,261	22,632	14,099	12,643
2006	39,500	26,311	22,286	17,138	12,135
sum	100,960	71,829	62,180	44,565	36,927

Added up the sum of all profits over the years 2000-2006 of the six companies was *$ 315.5 billion.*

Illustrative for this spectacular increase in profits is the fact that Exxon had $11.4 billion net profit in 2002, and Shell $9.7 billion in that same year. Cashflow is more than profit. The total cashflow generated by the five companies was a mega amount: $ 420.9 billion. These results were mainly due to the favourable oil and gas prices in those years. The economy was booming, especially in upcoming nations such as China and India. A sharply increasing demand for oil was the consequence of this, and there was an expectation of a further increase. There were also 'worries' about the availability of oil in the future.

It appears to be very rational to consider alternatives for fossil energy if you foresee an end to the availability. The huge amounts of cashflow generated in these years should have been invested in the development of new forms of energy.

Evidently the big five had other ideas about what to do with the cashflow. During the years 2004-2006 they invested less than 1% of the $ 420.9 billion in research and development of new energy sources, such as biofuel, water, wind and solar energy. Of course they invested mainly in oil and gas exploration and production techniques. Another area of great expense was in deep sea exploration (Gulf of Mexico, BP). The expenditure for these investments took approximately half of the $ 420.9 billion.

Even more remarkable than their investment strategy, is the attitude towards the shareholders. During 2004-2006 they paid out *$ 219.4 billion to their shareholders. The same amount as expended for investments.*

As shares in big corporations (PLCs) are at bearer, it is not traceable who the beneficiaries were of these huge amounts, unless the shareholders are other companies, banks, insurance companies, or pension funds. The big five paid out $ 94.9 billion as dividend, or 30% of their total net profits. Dividends are paid out pro rato of the number of shares held. All shareholders that held shares at the time dividends shared in the pay-out.

However, the oil companies also repurchased their own shares at a large scale, and paid the market price at the moment of transaction for it.

Exxon, for example, in 2005 repurchased 268 million shares at a total amount of $ 18.2 billion, and in 2006 401 million shares at a total of $ 29.6 billion. Over two years Exxon repurchased 10% of their shares outstanding. In 2005 Shell repurchased 157 million shares at $ 5 billion and in 2006 245 million at $ 8.2 billion.

Together the five corporations repurchased shares at a total amount of *$ 124.6 billion!* For the greater part it is completely unclear with whom the transactions were made. Bigger private shareholders who were for a long time holding their shares must have profited enormously from this.

Financial experts state that repurchasing own shares is only justified if there is a situation of surplus cash. This means, that the company has no better investment goals than buying back their own shares. It increases the earnings per share. It underlines the attitude of the oil companies towards new energy sources. If there had been real concerns about the future of fossil energy, one would have expected a different attitude.

The question why the big five were that generous towards their shareholders remains a mystery, as well as the question who were the unknown private beneficiaries of these huge amounts!

TINA AND TANIA

Oil and gas prices are increasing continuously. On the question why this happens, is subject to discussion:, even during the crisis, the parties involved point the accusing finger at each other. Various aspects influence this process. Governments of oil- producing countries require an ever increasing part of the revenues. Producing companies keep their capacity deliberately low, and refineries have processing constraints. Speculators gamble with future contracts on oil and push the price up. Governments of oil consuming countries require an ever increasing part of the oil revenues. Whatever the cause may be, all parties mentioned profit from a high oil price, and the consumer has to pay the price.

Although BP saw its profit decrease by 22%, this company was still generous to its shareholders. They expended an amount equal to the profit to keep them satisfied. Exxon equalled the mega result of 2006 in the succeeding year, with a net profit of $ 40 billion. This corporation paid out $ 8 billion dividend and repurchased shares at an amount of $ 33 billion in that year.

The Exxon annual report 2007 states that: *"Purchases may be made in both the **open market** and through **negotiated transactions**, and may be increased, decreased or discontinued at any time without prior notice."*

Shell made a profit of $ 31 billion in 2007, an increase of 24% compared to the year before. Shell paid $ 13 billion to its shareholders (dividends + repurchase). Shell was the least generous of the giants. Although the media messages suggest differently, Shell did not invest big amounts in R&D for the development of durable energy.

While Shell had to give up part of the ownership in new oil and gas fields, for example in Sachalin (Russia), they were forced to change their strategy more in the direction of new exploration and production techniques, to be applied in deep sea and Arctic areas. This is difficult and hazardous as we all found out through the spillage disaster in the Gulf of Mexico.

Oil spill disaster in the Gulf of Mexico

The continuously repeated story in the media that oil and gas will come to an end within a relatively few number of years, seems to be exaggerated. The truth is that countries such as Iran, Russia, and Venezuela 'hold their hand on the tap'. The big oil companies were used to dealing with willing and often corrupt governments. John Perkins is clear about this in *Confessions of an Economic Hitman*. It is all about geopolitical interests.

Shell, hit by this game, ventilated their grief in the media:

> 'The future energy sourcing can be characterised by two abbrevia-
> tions; TINA and TANIA. TINA stands for 'There is no alternative', TA-
> NIA for 'There are no ideal answers'. This is the gloomy conclusion
> of Vice President Jeremy Bentham of Shell Global Business Environ-
> ment in his presentation about energy scenarios until 2050.
> Energy hunger of China and India lead to an explosive growth of
> the demand for fossil energy. The consequence of an ever increas-
> ing world population is an ever increasing demand for oil and gas.
> The time of easy oil is gone.'
>
> SOURCE: HET FINANCIEELE DAGBLAD 12 FEBRUARY 2008

Big brother Exxon is joining Shell in their grief:

> Exxon Mobil's chairman Rex Tillerson criticized rich oil and gas pro-
> ducing countries that change contracts with oil and gas companies
> one-sided. Energy nationalism could have far reaching consequences
> for the world economy and the trustworthiness of energy supplies.
> Energy nationalism is contra productive, warned the CEO. If supplies
> are kept scarce by preventing foreign investments the world econo-
> my will slow down. Citizens of these countries pay the bill because
> investments in the domestic economy remain at a low level.
>
> SOURCE: HET FINANCIEELE DAGBLAD 13 NOVEMBER 2007

The lamentations of Shell and Exxon can be explained as moves on the
big geopolitical chessboard. However, the concerns about the future of
energy are ludicrous combined with their clear disinterest in the development of renewable energy on a large scale. The role of protector of
mankind does not suit them.

THE CHANGE IN MINDSET

Comparing the websites of the big oil corporations in 2006 and 2010 shows a shift from an apparent interest in renewable energy to a complete 'back to basics' strategy directed to exploration of oil and gas. Shell is crystal clear about this. On their website you can read: 'Our strategy seeks to reinforce our position as a leader in the oil and gas industry in order to provide a competitive shareholder return while helping to meet global energy demand in a responsible way'. Their investments are for the greater part in winning techniques like oil out of tar sands, deep sea drilling techniques and liquefying natural gas.

Exxon informs their shareholders in the 2009 annual report as follows:

> 'Over the next five years we will continue to invest record amounts, more than $ 125 billion to advance new technologies, deliver new upstream projects, increase production of higher-value refined products. ....For our upstream business, 2009 was a strong year. Eight major projects not only deliver new supplies of crude oil and natural gas to the world, but also provide significant value for our resource owners and for our shareholders.'

Both Exxon and Shell do not intend to become a green company in the sense of producing a material volume of renewable energy. What they do want is safe production techniques, more value out of the produced oil and gas, and advanced exploration techniques. It appears that the conclusion has been drawn; There Is No Alternative and There Are No Ideal Answers. TINA and TANIA formulated by Shell in 2007 have established themselves firmly in the minds of the energy thinkers.

Yet, TINA and TANIA are self-fulfilling prophecies. As long as year after year the capital-intensive corporations fail to invest more than marginal amounts in the development of renewable energy, and instead prefer to pamper their shareholders, there is no real chance for renewable energy to become a realistic alternative.

In fact it is the same story as with banks. In the end the taxpayer has to pay the bill. For example, in 2009 Germany's government formulated a very ambitious plan to increase the contribution of renewable energy in the total electric energy consumption to at least 30% by 2020. In 2007, this share was still 14%. Also by 2020 at least 14% of the heating of buildings and houses in Germany should be supplied by renewable energy, for example through solar energy, and heat pumps. (Source: Ministry of Economic Affairs Germany)

Even this ambitious plan will supply just a minority share in the total energy consumption. And big investments are needed by the German government. This money, that is not available, due to the developments surrounding the Euro (the problems with the state debts of Portugal, Ireland, Italy, Greece, and Spain), the low economy, and the continuing problems in the financial sector. The pressure on the German government is immense, as they play the role of cart-horse in the European Union. No wonder that one year later, in March 2010, at a conference in Kassel, Germany's biggest oil and gas company announced an intensified search for newly to be exploited oil- and gas, without mentioning climate change or, renewable energy whatsoever.

There are various other international examples of the turn away from renewable energy. Also because of governmental budget problems the international nuclear fusion project Iter was stopped in 2009. In France the plan to tax CO2 emissions has been dropped. In the UK the mindset was changed after an alarming report from the OFGEM (energy supervising institute), warning against an energy crisis if the hopes were set too high for renewable energy. Two more examples underline the changed attitude of the German and British governments because of budget constraints:

The German government today agreed to extend the working lives of its nuclear reactors by an average of 12 years, in a controversial move that will shape the energy strategy of Europe's largest nation for decades to come.

Having put the seal on a deal that was hammered out after lengthy talks between politicians and power companies, the German chancellor, Angela Merkel , hailed it as a "revolution in energy provision". She said it would help to ensure Germany's place at the forefront of "the most environmentally and worldwide most efficient" energy policy.

Under the agreement, the four power companies E.ON, RWE, EnBW and Vattenfall have agreed to pay the German government €30bn (£25bn) to allow the operating lives of its 17 nuclear plants to be extended. The companies will also pay €2.3bn in nuclear-fuel rods tax over the next six years, as well as an annual €300m for the next two years and €200m between 2013 and 2016 into a special renewable energy investment fund. The decision marks a turnaround on the decision reached almost a decade ago under the Social Democratic (SPD) and Green party coalition of Gerhard Schröder to phase out nuclear power early in the next decade. Opposition politicians and environmental groups referred to today variously as "heartbreaking" and "a black day".

SOURCE: THE GUARDIAN, 30 AUGUST 2010

The U.K. government will this month (September 2010) sound the death knell for the world's largest tidal energy project – to be built across the Severn estuary between Somerset and south Wales – when it rules out public funding for the controversial £20bn plan. The announcement will please some environmentalists, who were worried about the impact on bird life in the estuary, but others say such spending cuts will make a mockery of David Cameron's pledge to be the "greenest government ever". The private sector is unlikely to back the 10-mile tidal barrage, which would be able to provide 5% of the UK's electricity, without government money.

SOURCE: THE GUARDIAN, 5 SEPTEMBER 2010

Governments may see the need of the development of renewable energy in the interest of the future and for the world we leave to our children, yet they are very limited in what they can do because of budget constraints.

Econcern, a Dutch medium-sized company developing and producing durable energy has become a victim of the lack of government support. This company was active in solar-, wind, and bio energy. The company was praised as the forerunner of the post-fossil energy era. In 2008 the chairman of this company was proclaimed Dutch CEO of the year. Barely three months later the debts were too high for the company to be able to survive. What happened? Investments of the types done by Econcern have generally a long pay-back period. Investors in Econcern should therefore be patient. Initially the enthusiasm of private investors and banks was big. Investing in Econcern was investing in the future. However, the change in attitude towards durable energy also affected the minds of the Econcern investors. Doubts arose, and after an audit the company appeared to be in an organizational and financial chaos. The investors withdrew, and the financial problems became obviously unbridgeable. Initially the Dutch government was willing to give financial support to Econcern. However, this support was never given a concrete form. Econcern disappeared via the backstage.

The financial struggle of renewable energy companies is not typically Dutch. This example shows a similar case in the U.S.:

> EPV, a U.S. New Jersey based designer, developer, manufacturer and marketer of low amorphous silicon ("a-Si") thin-film photovoltaic solar modules, voluntarily filed for chapter 11 bankruptcy protection on Wednesday. The company was founded in 1991, but its troubles primarily began with a 2007 decision to implement "a plan to expand production capacity to facilitate the manufacture and sale of larger quantities of modules and began to design, manufacture

and sell high-performance, low-cost a-Si thin-film PV modules to customers in a variety of end markets, particularly customers building large solar fields." In connection with that strategy, EPV issued $77.5 million in senior secured convertible notes maturing in June 2010. The company also reports that it entered into "long-term supply contracts with numerous customers for sales anticipated to exceed $1 billion over the terms of the contracts (generally five to six years)."

Those sales never materialized, as they were connected to the construction of large solar farms which never got built because financing was not available for the projects. This was especially problematic for EPV because its contracts did not contain minimum order volumes or cancellation penalties (which EPV states was consistent with standard industry contract terms). In an attempt to shore up its balance sheet, EPV was successful in July 2009 in getting holders of approximately 50% of the 2007 notes to exchange their notes for equity, warrants and $50 million in new notes. However, EPVs business continued to deteriorate and it ceased manufacturing operations and laid off 350 employees (only 24 remain as of Wednesday's bankruptcy filing).

SOURCE: WWW.NETDOCKETSBLOG.COM

The examples underline how TINA and TANIA have become self-fulfilling prophecies, and that unless the citizens of the western countries put a lot of pressure on their governments to change the attitude towards renewable energy, we will remain in the hands of the 'fossils'. Of course it also proves that governments measure by at least two standards. Failing banks are supported financially with huge amounts, relatively small amounts to support innovative businesses, important for our future, are simply denied.

CHAPTER 4

A concise history
of money

'I believe that banking institutions are more dangerous than stand-
ing armies.....

If the American people ever allow private banks to control the issue
of currency... the banks and corporations that will grow up around
them will deprive the people of their property until their children
wake up homeless on the continent their fathers conquered.'

THOMAS JEFFERSON (1743 – 1826)

Basically money is no more than a medium of exchange. Shells, amber, ivory, precious stones have been used all over the world and still are in use in some areas. Bartering of commodities appeared to be too difficult. For example, if I had some strawberries for sale and wanted to exchange them for a loaf of bread, what would happen if the baker didn't like strawberries? I would have to find someone who is willing to sell me something the baker wants for my strawberries. This example explains the existence of money as a medium of exchange. If money had remained just a medium of exchange, the world would have been less complex than it is nowadays.

When did money start to be a thing that could be bought and sold? Presumably, around 4000 BC in Sumer. In that era the practice of lending money to citizens in the temples started. The temple was the place where the gods were worshipped, so the first bankers were temple priests. They calculated extreme interest percentages, sometimes as much as 33.3%. People became heavily in debt, and many would not have managed to survive if there had not been the so-called Jubilee year. In a Jubilee year all debts were let off. This phenomenon has existed for ages, and in more cultures. For example the Jews had a Jubilee year every 49 years. Also the Sumer and Babylon kings were in debt to the temples just like the citizens. In ancient times religion exerted vast powers over kings and citizens through money. No wonder that the privilege to issue money has always been a very important subject. Proof of the importance to have control over the issue of money is the following quote from one of the most notorious bankers in history:

> "Let me issue and control a nation's money and I care not who writes the laws."
>
> MAYER AMSCHEL ROTHSCHILD, 1790

The majority of us are not aware of this, and this is largely due to the fact that the winning side increasingly continues to be a vital and respected member of our global society, having influence over large aspects of our lives including our education, our media and our governments.

While we might feel powerless in trying to stop issuing money for private profit at our expense, it is easy to forget that we collectively give money its value. We have first been taught to believe that gold or silver coins with the head of an emperor or king on it and on the flip side some lines that suggest a kind of metaphysical nature had the value suggested by the issuers of them. Later we came to believe that printed pieces of paper have special value, and because we know others believe this too, we are willing to work all our lives to get what we are convinced others will want. In reality we are kept as slaves by the issuers of money, who make us believe that the real value of our efforts is in coins and printed paper instead of in the goods and services we produce. The difficult thing is we have already been, for thousands of years reliable co-players in the game directed by the issuers of money or financial elite, as I will call them from now on.

Early Christianity rejected making money with money. Evidence of this can be found in the story about Jesus and the money changers in the temple. The money changers misused their position as the only sellers of silver shekels. People had to pay their tax with those coins because it was the only one acceptable to God. The price they paid for the silver shekel was driven up by the money changers. Jesus drove them out with a whip, shouting they were 'a den of thieves'. Making money over the backs of naive people was blasphemy in His eyes. What the money exchangers did was clearly a practice exercised long before Christ. Jesus' holy anger about usury was surely based on the power exerted by those who issued money over man.

In the middle ages Christians still rejected usury. Thomas Aquinas (1247) stated:

> "To take interest for money lent is unjust in itself, because this is to sell what does not exist, and this evidently leads to inequality, which is contrary to justice.
>
> *Now, money was invented chiefly for the purpose of exchange.*

> Hence, it is by its very nature unlawful to take payment for the use
> of money lent, which payment is known as interest."

Yet in medieval times the stage was set for banking as we know it in present time.

Goldsmiths offered people to keep their gold and silver safe in their vaults. To have proof of their ownership they received receipts from the goldsmith. These receipts soon became popular for trade as gold and silver were heavy to carry, and there was the constant threat of robbery. Only a small part of the depositors came in to demand their gold. Clever goldsmiths realised that they could lend out money that was not covered by gold or silver. Of course people that borrowed this money paid interest to the goldsmith. This is how fractional reserve banking came into existence. In fact, as you can see it was based on fraud.

Also as in the old Sumer days the church played an important role in the making of money by money industry, despite what the basic idea of Christians was about interest. For example in medieval times the Templars were known as bankers. All over Europe and in the Middle East they had a network of what might be called bank offices. Travelling salesman could deposit their valuables with them, and receive a letter that served as money elsewhere. The Vatican Bank is still one of the major financial institutes in the world.

Today banks are allowed to loan out at least ten times the amount they are actually holding, so while you wonder how they get rich charging you 10% interest, it's not 10% a year they make on that amount but actually 96%. This works as follows: A new banker has put 1,000 euro in cash. Because he has a banking license he can consequently lend out 9,000 euro. Money created out of thin air. The banker receives 900 euro interest per year (10% over 9,000). His return on investment then is 900/1,000 = 90%. The idea that banks are just an intermediate between savers and borrowers is false. An analysis of the Balance sheets of the largest 100 banks you will confirm this.

At the same time other money systems existed everywhere in Europe, like the 'kerfstok' in The Netherlands, and the tally sticks in England. The ingenious tally stick invented during the reign of King Henry I (12th century) survived for more than 700 years. It proved that as long as people are willing to accept a medium of exchange as money it actually works. The tally stick was made of polished wood, with notches cut along one edge to signify the denominations. The stick was then split full length so each piece still had a record of the notches. The issuer kept one half for proof against counterfeiting, and then spent the other half into the market place where it would continue to circulate as money. Because only tally sticks were accepted by the rulers of the land for payment of taxes, there was a built-in demand for them, which gave people confidence to accept these as money.

Presumably King Henry invented the tally stick to remain out of the hands of the upcoming goldsmith bankers' class. It also explains why people forgot about the tally stick, after the Bank of England was established in 1694. This Bank has been a private enterprise from the beginning, with private shareholders. The tally stick money system was from the start of the Bank of England considered as a rival, and wiped away as being a primitive and unworkable system. The strategy to get rid of the tally stick system was simply to pretend it never existed and not to discuss it. And clearly the strategy has worked.

The shareholders of the Bank of England whose names were kept secret, were meant to invest one and a quarter million pounds, but only three quarters of a million was received when it was chartered in 1694 and from that year on fractional reserve banking bloomed. Money was lent out many times more than it had in reserve, collecting interest on the lot, all in the interest of the shareholders. Even the Bank of England's nationalisation in 1946 is not what it at first may appear, as its independent resources unceasingly multiply and dividends continue to be produced for its shareholders. The establishment of the Bank of England was the jewel in the crown of the goldsmith bankers, the inventors of fractional reserve banking. Through the ages this financial elite grew ever more powerful. The purchase of the square mile called the City of London in the seventeenth century proved their increasing power. For centuries The City was the financial centre of the world. This position shifted to Wall Street after World War II.

You might think someone would have seen through this, and realised how on earth they could produce their own money and owe no interest, but instead the Bank of England has been used as a model and now nearly every nation has a Central Bank with fractional reserve banking at its core.

This is how it works: A country sells bonds to the bank in return for money it cannot raise in taxes. The bonds are paid for by money *'produced from thin air'*. The government pays interest on the money it borrowed by borrowing more money in the same way. There is no way this debt can ever be paid, it has and will continue to increase. If the government did find a way to pay off the debt, the result would be that there would be no bonds to back the currency, so to pay the debt would be to kill the currency. The statement that money only exists through debt is clearly true! The consequence of this is that the money supply keeps on growing. Inflation and increasing prices follow the ever bigger money supplies.

Until a financial crisis hits us............

The resemblance between the Jubilee year and a financial crisis is striking. In the Jubilee year debts were let off. In times of financial crisis money becomes scarce, businesses go bankrupt, and people lose their jobs. In a financial crisis debts also disappear, however together with private property. It leaves many people homeless, jobless, and poor.

You might say that a financial crisis is a negative translation of the real meaning of the Jubilee year.

Yet as hard as it might be to believe, in times of economic crises wealth is rarely destroyed and instead is often only transferred. When the majority of people are suffering through economic depression, you can be sure that a minority of people are continuing to get rich.

Central Banks all over the world show continuously their determination to prevent crises, yet there have been nothing but crises and instability over the past 300 years. One thing, however, has been stable and that is the growing fortune of the Rothschild's.

A goldsmith named Amschel Moses Bauer opened a counting house in Frankfurt Germany in 1743. He placed a Roman eagle on a red shield over the door prompting people to call his shop the Red Shield Firm pronounced in German as "Rothschild". His son later changed his name to Rothschild when he inherited the business. Lending money to individuals was all well and good but he soon found it much more profitable loaning money to governments and kings. Remember the old days of Sumer and Babylon? The loans involved much bigger amounts and were secured by public taxes that the kings imposed on their subjects. Amshell transferred his experience in and vision on the art of money creation out of thin air to his five sons, before sending them out to the major financial centres of the world to create new banks and dominate the already existing central banking systems. The Rothschilds were the driving force behind the establishment of Central Banks in the main capitals of Europe.

J.P. Morgan was thought by many to be the richest man in the world during the second world war, but upon his death it was discovered he was merely a lieutenant within the Rothschild empire owning only 19% of the J.P. Morgan Companies.

The decisive role that the financial elite played is well illustrated by the way things went in the British colonies in North America.

By the mid 1700s Britain was at its height of power, but was also heavily in debt. Since the creation of the Bank of England, they had suffered four costly wars and the total debt now stood at £140,000,000, (which in those days was a lot of money). In order to cover the debts the British government raised high amounts of taxes from the colonies. However because there was a shortage of material for minting coins in the colonies they were not able or willing to fulfil their obligations. In order to keep the economy going, the colonial government began to print their own paper money, which they called Colonial Script. This provided a very successful means of exchange and also gave the colonies a sense of their own identity. Colonial Script was money provided to help the exchange of goods. It was 'debt free' paper money not backed by gold or silver. In those years the economy in the colonies prospered as never before. During a visit to Britain in 1763 Benjamin Franklin was asked how he would account for the new found prosperity in the colonies. Franklin replied:

> "That is simple. In the colonies we issue our own money. It is called Colonial Script. We issue it in proper proportion to the demands of trade and industry to make the products pass easily from the producers to the consumers. In this manner, creating for ourselves our own paper money, we control its purchasing power, and we have no interest to pay to no one."

The colonies in North America had learned, as with the tally sticks centuries before, that people's confidence in the currency was all they needed, and they could be free of borrowing debts. In Response the privately owned Bank of England used its influence on the British Parliament to press for the passing of the Currency Act of 1764. This act made it illegal for the colonies to print their own money, and forced them to pay all future taxes to Britain in silver or gold.

Here is what Franklin said after that:

> "In one year, the conditions were so reversed that the era of prosperity ended, and a depression set in, to such an extent that the streets of the Colonies were filled with unemployed."

> "The colonies would gladly have borne the little tax on tea and other matters had it not been that England took away from the colonies their money, which created unemployment and dissatisfaction. The inability of the colonists to get power to issue their own money permanently out of the hands of George III and the international bankers was the PRIME reason for the Revolutionary War."

SOURCE: BENJAMIN FRANKLIN'S AUTOBIOGRAPHY

The last decades of the 18th century and the complete 19th century show a bitter struggle between the leaders of the new Republic of the United States of America and the financial elite. The first quote in this chapter from the third President Thomas Jefferson gives proof of this. Several times the financial elite tried to establish a Central Bank based on the Bank of England model. Strong leaders such as Andrew Jackson resisted the intrigues of the financial elite. He also survived more attempts on his life. Under President Abraham Lincoln the American government issued, similar to the colonial script, debt free currency known as *the greenback dollar.* There were moments when it appeared that they would not succeed, nevertheless the finest hour for the financial elite came in 1913, when the Federal Reserve Bank (FED) was established.

The name 'Federal Reserve' is misleading. The bank is not Federal, suggesting that it is working in public interest, it is privately owned, and it is run purely to gain profit for its private shareholders. The FED was established in a somewhat very sneaky way. On 23 December 1913 the senate did not give their consent to the Federal Reserve Act. Though most members of the senate had left for the Christmas holidays, due to a 'technical mistake' the senate was still in charge. There were only three members left, and they voted in favour of the Act unanimously.

> Rep. Charles Lindbergh: "The financial system has been turned over to... the federal reserve board. That board administers the finance system by authority of... a purely profiteering group. The system is private, conducted for the sole purpose of obtaining the greatest possible profits from the use of other peoples money."

> Rep. Louis T. McFadden:"We have in this country one of the most corrupt institutions the world has ever known. I refer to the Federal Reserve Board... This evil institution has impoverished... the people of the United States... and has practically bankrupted our Government. It has done this through... the corrupt practice of the moneyed vultures who control it."

These crystal clear statements speak for themselves.

Not only the American leaders, also Napoleon Bonaparte and the Russian Tsar resisted the growing power of the financial elite. This is a quote from Napoleon about bankers:

> "When a government is dependent upon bankers for money, they and not the leaders of the government control the situation, since the hand that gives is above the hand that takes... Money has no motherland; financiers are without patriotism and without decency; their sole object is gain."

In order to escape the grip of the financial elite Napoleon sold Louisiana to the U.S. for three million dollars in gold. With this amount he financed his wars against Britain, Austria, Prussia, and, finally, Russia. For both sides of a war to be lent money from the same privately owned Central Bank is not unusual. Nothing generates debt like war. A nation will borrow any amount to win. So naturally if the loser is kept going to the last straw in a vain hope of winning, then the more resources will be used up by the winning side before their victory is obtained more resources used, more loans taken out, more money made by the bankers; and even more amazingly, the loans are usually given on condition that the victor pays the debts left by the loser.

When Napoleon finally met his Waterloo the 'English' Nathan Rothschild did perhaps the most infamous thing in financial history. He misused foreknowledge with regard to the outcome of the battle at Waterloo. Though he knew that Wellington had won, he pretended that Britain had lost, causing a huge downfall at the London Stock Exchange by selling his stocks. Consequently, after the panic was complete and the shares were no more than a fraction of their value one day earlier, he swiftly bought back all available shares. One day later the news of Britain's victory came........

The 19th century became known as the age of the Rothschilds when it was estimated they controlled half of the world's wealth. While their wealth continues to increase today, they have managed to blend into the background, giving an impression that their power has waned. They only apply the Rothschild name to a small fraction of the companies they actually control.

The financial elite gained control over the issue of money through central banks. Where they were established, for instance, in Austria, France, Germany, The Netherlands, France, and Belgium, the idea of a government-based organisation of the financial system was firmly set. The image was respectable, solid, integer ('Safe as the Bank of England'). In reality central banks were in private hands. Governments borrowed huge amounts, and were heavily in debt with their central banks. Especially in times of war the money business prospered enormously. The German central bank for example lent money to the German government to finance the wars they fought in the late 19th century and world war I. The British central bank in its turn financed the many wars they fought in the 19th and 20th century. The French central bank did the same, etc. And all interest revenues were for the shareholders of the respective central banks. Those shareholders were as may now be clear, very small in numbers. It may also be clear that people that gain immense profits from human misery will stop at nothing. Strong leaders of any country who tried to escape from their grip could count on bitter opposition putting their own lives at risk.

"Power from any source tends to create an appetite for additional power... It was almost inevitable that the super-rich would one day aspire to control not only their own wealth, but the wealth of the whole world.

To achieve this, they were perfectly willing to feed the ambitions of the power-hungry political conspirators who were committed to

> the overthrow of all existing governments and the establishments
> of a central world-wide dictatorship."

W.CLEON SKOUSEN IN *THE NAKED CAPITALIST*

No wonder that the very same financial elite was also involved in financing the Nazis in the thirties of the last century. Anthony Sutton gives shocking evidence of this in his book *Wall Street and the rise of Hitler*.

Why is the money system, developed by the financial elite so devastating? The main reasons for that are:

- Fractional banking, that is creating money out of thin air based on a marginal reserve originally in gold (gold standard), in modern times based on money out of thin air.
- Placing governments, businesses, and private households in a debt position by treating money as a commodity that can be sold and bought instead of a medium of exchange.
- Varying the money supply at will, thereby causing financial and economic crisis repeatedly. Loan contracts can be ended and new loans denied if bankers think this is necessary. In times of crises many people lose their property and their jobs. At the same time the rich become richer.
- Creating debts of mega proportions that never can be paid off, leading to even more money and debt to 'help' the economy. In August 2010 the Federal Reserve Bank in the U.S. purchased a vast amount of government debt (treasury bonds), and increased the money supply at the same time. The money supply stood already at an all-time high level.

Nowadays we are so used to this money system that most people believe that there is no other solution. The memory of the Colonial Script, Tally Sticks, Greenback dollars etc. has been wiped out. Yet governments all over the world should realise that they could serve their citizens better by no longer playing part in the money game of the financial elite. Money issued on a debt free basis by governments themselves instead of borrowing it from banks could be the beginning of a new era, where there is prosperity for everyone, and not for just a small number of people.

It is as President Abraham Lincoln stated it:

> "The government should create, issue and circulate all the currency and credit needed to satisfy the spending power of the government and the buying power of consumers..... The privilege of creating and issuing money is not only the supreme prerogative of Government, but it is the Government's greatest creative opportunity. By the adoption of these principles, the long-felt want for a uniform medium will be satisfied. The taxpayers will be saved immense sums of interest, discounts and exchanges. The financing of all public enterprises, the maintenance of stable government and ordered progress, and the conduct of the Treasury will become matters of practical administration. The people can and will be furnished with a currency as safe as their own government. Money will cease to be the master and become the servant of humanity. Democracy will rise superior to the money power."

The by many wished for return to the Gold Standard nowadays is not a real improvement. It just means playing the card the financial elite likes to play. Gold is a relatively rare commodity, and can therefore be monopolised easily. Returning to the gold standard implies that those who possess gold are placed in the centre of power more than ever. The biographies of all the Wall Street 'giants', J.P. Morgan, Joe F. Kennedy, J.D Rockefeller, Bernard Baruch, Henry Ford, all marvel at how they got out of the stock market and put their assets in 'gold' just before the crash of 1929.

In reality the rich received a secret directive, sent by the father of the Federal Reserve Bank, Paul Warburg, warning of the coming collapse and depression.

With control of the press and the education system, few Americans are aware that the Fed caused the depression. It is however a well known fact among leading top economists.

"The Federal Reserve definitely caused the Great depression by contracting the amount of currency in circulation by one-third from 1929 to 1933."

THE GREAT CONTRACTION 1929-1933, MILTON FRIEDMAN, NOBEL PRIZE WINNING ECONOMIST

Another evidence of the love of gold by the financial elite is the following true story. In 1933 new President Franklin D. Roosevelt signed a bill forcing all the American people to hand over all their gold at a $ 20 per ounce base rate, with the exception of rare coins. People who would not comply risked a long time in jail. Bought at this bargain price with money out of thin air produced by the Federal Reserve, the gold was melted down and transported to Fort Knox. There are people that witnessed about the endless long trains in the direction of Fort Knox. Consequently in 1935 the price of gold was raised from $20 up to $35 per ounce. Furthermore, gold could be bought by non-Americans only for that price. This meant those who had avoided the crash by investing in gold they had shipped to London could now nearly double their money while the rest of America starved. Also the financial elite, that has as Napoleon stated no patriotism, were able to buy huge amounts of gold from the American government at a relatively low price. And apparently they did.

In 1945 Fort Knox did officially hold 70% of the world's gold. However, over the years it was said to be sold off to the financial elite. A public audit of Fort Knox reserves was repeatedly denied. Rumours spread about missing gold.

> Allegations of missing gold from our Fort Knox vaults are being widely discussed in European circles. But what is puzzling is that the Administration is not hastening to demonstrate conclusively that there is no cause for concern over our gold treasure - if indeed it is in a position to do so.
>
> EDITH ROOSEVELT

When at last in 1981 under President Ronald Reagan a Gold Commission was installed to reconsider a gold standard, they found that the US Treasury owned no gold at all.

Over six thousand years since the era of Sumer, today's money system has remained practically the same with the difference only that the humane aspect with the Jubilee year has disappeared. Today's financial elite has no compassion whatsoever with their fellow man. The only driving force appears to be an insatiable hunger for more power and more possessions.

Reforming the banking system will not help. Governments should take their responsibility and care for their citizens by democratising the creation of money completely, and remove the right to issue money from the bankers. Should they fail to do so, the only thing we as common people can do is to restore the trust in money as purely an medium of exchange by introducing complementary currencies in a diversity that cannot be controlled by any power. Luckily there are already people all over the world who have understood this urge, and created all kinds of regional solutions.

SOURCES CONSULTED FOR THIS CHAPTER:

The History of money, 2009, Jack Weatherford

A History of Money and Banking in the United States, the Colonial Era to World

War II, 2002, Murray N. Rothbard

History of Money from Ancient Times to the Present Day, 2005, Glen Davies

History of Money in the British empire & the United States, 2010, Agnes F. Dodd

Money as Debt I, 2007, Paul Grignon (available on DVD), and Money as Debt II 2010, Paul Grignon (available on DVD)

Der Mythos vom Geld-Die Geschichte der Macht. Vom Tauschhandel zum Euro: eine Geschichte des Geldes und der Wahrungen, 1999, Stephen Zarlenga

The French Connection, The History of the House of Rothschild, 2007, Andrew Hitchcock (digital)

CHAPTER 5

The post WWII monetary regime

In 1944 the western allies in World War II came together to discuss the organization of the postwar monetary system. The international monetary regime that was agreed upon took place in Bretton Woods. The main reason for the Bretton Woods agreement was the complete failure of the intended international cooperation after the end of World War I. There were many arguments for the allies to make sure that there would be no recurrence the things that went wrong during the interwar period. Things that went wrong were amongst others the Great Depression that started in 1929 and lasted for more than a decade, the instability of the international monetary situation during all of the interwar years, the poverty in Germany due to the gigantic sums of money this country had to pay to the victors of WWI, and the isolationistic economic policies of the biggest economies in that era.

The Bretton Woods regime was a monetary system to govern currency relations among sovereign states. The International Monetary Fund

(IMF) was intended to have supranational authority in order to make multilateral decision making on monetary matters between more countries possible. The IMF was and is meant to be an multi-national institute to serve the well-being of the world economy. In practice the United States had a decisive influence in the IMF, because the U.S. was the biggest donor, particularly during the first decades of its existence. Therefore the IMF acted mainly according to the wishes and will of the biggest financial and economic power after the war.

Due to two successive wars Great Britain was bankrupt at the end of WWII, Germany was completely devastated, and the other European countries were in a bad state. As I wrote in Chapter 4, the British dominant financial position was finished in 1945. Wall Street became the new financial centre of the world. The United States enforced their hegemony by imposing on their allies that the dollar was going to be the world reserve currency, as good as gold. Another big advantage for the position of the dollar as World reserve currency was and is, the fact that important commodities like oil, airplanes etc. are traded in dollars. Therefore demand for dollars was and still is not only generated by the U.S. itself but also by countries all over the world. This helped the dominant position of the U.S. in the world economy a lot.

John Maynard Keynes, the famous economist, tried to introduce the "Bancor" as the world currency unit. Although the thought of one world currency appears to be attractive and might have been a better solution than the dollar as world reserve unit, there are many disadvantages to it. Our experience with the euro provides proof of that. Moreover and foremost, a world currency in a money system governed by the same old financial elite is a recipe for a lot of trouble as was pointed out in Chapter Four above. Dollars were to be the pivot around which all other currencies were spinning in a 'pegged rate' to the dollar. (Members were required to establish a parity of their national currencies in terms of gold (a "peg") and to maintain exchange rates within plus or minus 1% of parity (a "band"). 'As good as gold' was literally, that dollars were exchangeable for gold at a fixed rate of $ 35 per ounce. By the way, the same price as set by Roosevelt in 1935! And we know that in 1933 the U.S. treasury had been filled with a lot of gold, 'bought' from American citizens. Only central banks of the member countries (there were 43 member countries in the Bretton Woods agreement) were allowed to exchange gold for dollars and dollars for gold at the fixed rate of $ 35 per ounce. Private investors and businesses had to buy gold on the open market, where the price was formed by demand and supply.

The other institute that played and still plays an important role in postwar global finance is the World Bank. The World Bank was to be a specialized agency of the United Nations charged with making loans for economic development purposes.

The Oxford dictionary of business writes about the World Bank:

> A specialized agency working in coordination with the United Nations, established in 1945 to help finance postwar reconstruction and to help raise standards of living in developing countries, by making loans to governments or guaranteeing outside loans. It lends on broadly commercial terms, either for specific projects or for more general social purposes; funds are raised on the international capital markets. The World Bank is owned by the governments of 151 countries. Members must also be members of the International Monetary Fund. The headquarters of the Bank are in Washington, with a European office in Paris and a Tokyo office.

Europe was, as I mentioned before, in a bad state after World War II. There was a lack of practically everything. Food, clothing, machinery, you name it. Much of these goods had to be imported from the United States. The consequence of this was an ever growing debt from the European countries, and this would have killed the reconstruction of the European economy if there had not been The Marshall Plan. The new

IMF in consortium with the World Bank were incapable of solving the problem, due to lack of capital. This a quote from a speech by George Marshall (ex.U.S.Secretary of State) in 1947:

> The breakdown of the business structure of Europe during the war was complete. ...Europe's requirements for the next three or four years of foreign food and other essential products... principally from the United States... are so much greater than her present ability to pay that she must have substantial help or face economic, social and political deterioration of a very grave character.

From 1948 to 1954 the United States provided 16 Western European countries with $17 billion in grants. Of course the bad economic situation in Germany after World War I, due to the immense payments that country had to make to the victors of WWI, opening the door for Hitler, and the growing influence of communism, were the main reasons for this help. The United States would have lost an important market and a lot of money because of debts that would never have been paid off. Yet, in the constant mixture of good and bad, there was undoubtedly something good in the Marshall Plan. The economic recovery in the countries that were approved by the Truman doctrine (ex. U.S. president Truman, who considered communism as the biggest threat of his time) speeded up rapidly.

> To encourage long-term adjustment, the United States promoted European and Japanese trade competitiveness. Policies for economic controls on the defeated former Axis countries (Germany, Italy, Japan) were scrapped. Aid to Europe and Japan was designed to rebuild productivity and export capacity. In the long run it was expected that such European and Japanese recovery would benefit the United States by widening markets for U.S. exports, and providing locations for U.S. capital expansion.

WIKIPEDIA

The markets the U.S. had in mind developed indeed. By the mid-sixties the newly formed European Economic Community and Japan had become respectable international economic powers. Their per capita income and economic growth surpassed that of the U.S. Of course this caused tension between the new economic powers and the U.S., until then the undisputed strongest economy in the world. The Bretton Woods regime also came under constant pressure, especially because of the coupling of dollars and gold. There was simply not enough gold available to be able to keep the promise to exchange dollars for gold by the central banks of the E.E.C. countries and Japan. Furthermore, the U.S. constantly increased their dollars money supply by issuing more and more dollars, amongst others to finance their expensive wars, like in Vietnam and big domestic projects such as the Great Society program for which ex-US President L.B. Johnson refused to raise taxes. An increasing money supply means devaluation of the currency, which in fact did happen with the dollar. This to the dissatisfaction of the new economic powers who had more and more problems with the dollar as world reserve currency, because it led to an overvaluing of the dollar at the cost of currencies such as the yen and the deutschmark.

Ex-US President R. Nixon ended the 'as good as gold' promise in 1971. He "closed the gold window", making the dollar inconvertible to gold directly, except on the open market. Unusually, this decision was made without consulting members of the international monetary system or even his own State Department, and was soon dubbed the Nixon Shock. With this one-sided act Bretton Woods was dead. Many bilateral conferences under U.S. leadership were necessary to form a new multilateral monetary regime, sometimes called Bretton Woods II, although the recent financial crisis has proven that nowadays there is no such thing as a well operating international monetary system. Since 1971 there have been the repeatedly held conferences of the G8 and sometimes the G20 (the most powerful economies in the world). We all know from experience the lack of decision making power of these conferences. This is logical, because the real powers remain hidden, as

I have explained earlier. The G20 have proven to be unable to tackle the important issues effectively. Also the way the 20 most powerful economic powers have responded to the present financial crisis until now proves the lack of real cooperation. It is in reality 'together for ourselves'.

Protest against bail-out of banks in the U.S.

This is part of a report of the G20 summit April 2009, published in the British newspaper *The Guardian*.

> Gordon Brown today claimed that the end of the global recession was now achievable as he unveiled an agreement from the G20 summit that will pump an additional $1tn (£748bn) into the world economy. "Today's decisions, of course, will not immediately solve the crisis. But we have begun the process by which it will be solved," Brown added.

Brown said that the ability of the G20 countries to work together in this way showed that the era when global finance was dominated by the so-called "Washington consensus" was over.

"I think a new world order is emerging with the foundation of a new progressive era of international cooperation," Brown said.

- The injection of an additional $1tn into the global economy through measures including a $500bn increase in the funding available to the IMF, an increase in the availability of money for developing countries through the IMF's "special drawing rights" to $250bn and a total of $250bn being set aside for trade assistance
- Reform of institutions such as the IMF to allow countries like China to have greater influence. Senior posts at the IMF and the World Bank will open to candidates from the developing world.
- Renewed commitment to the millennium development goals.
- $50bn for the world's poorest countries.

The world came together to fight against the global recession".

The G20 countries will also beef up the Financial Stability Forum – the Basel-based grouping of central bankers, finance ministries and national regulators – giving it sweeping new powers to oversee the world's financial markets. Re-named the Financial Stability Board, the body, which now includes all the G20 countries, as well as the original G8 members, will coordinate action *across international borders.*

The only thing that happened in the past few years is that governments have injected a lot of money issued out of thin air into the economy, to stimulate it and foremost, to save the banks. Seemingly the effort to save the banks has been successful, but at what cost? Moreover, has it improved the monetary situation? If the system remains unchanged and if those who are pulling the ropes stay in charge, nothing really changes in a positive way. I will come back to this in a later chapter.

In the fifties and sixties of the last century there was the monetary hegemony of the U.S. In the following decades until recently the U.S. managed to maintain their position in the core, though more and more challenged by the economic powers Japan and E.E.C.. And in the past two decades China has rapidly become more influential in the select group. Gordon Brown suggested in his speech at the G20 summit that a 'new world order' is emerging based on international cooperation. Maybe there are developments on a higher level in international politics. Yet there is still little evidence of the new world order he talked about.

The role that will be given to the Financial Stability Board is apparently one of big influence on the future monetary system. This will be discussed further in the Chapter 'The Bank for International Settlements'. The financial elite, discussed in chapter three always chooses the winning side. Today this is Asia, particularly China:

> Global asset manager The Carlyle Group announced on 3 August 2010 the first closing of its RMB Fund, which is now ready to invest. The RMB Fund, which has a target size of RMB 5 billion (approximately US$740 million), will make investments in large growth companies in Beijing and across China. Carlyle has received more than RMB2.4 billion (approximately US$350 million) in commitments from a variety of sources, including: Beijing State-owned Capital Operation and Management Center (BSCOMC), Beijing Equity Investment Development Fund, as well as other large SOEs, private companies and individuals.
>
> SOURCE: WWW.CARLYLE.COM/MEDIA ROOM/NEWS ARCHIVE/2010/ITEM11054.HTML

As from 1971 the worldwide monetary system entered into a downward sliding scale. Over the past decades the money supply has increased enormously. And as a consequence of this, the value of money has decreased dramatically. Evidence of this process is found in the ever increasing commodity prices. For example, nowadays in The Netherlands you need a disposable income of € 60,000 to buy the same commodities one could buy in 1970 with a disposable income of € 10,000.

One major conclusion may be that as long as there was the undisputed leadership of the U.S., there was a kind of stability that might be described as the Pax Americana referring to the Pax Romana in ancient times. When the U.S. leadership was challenged, stability disappeared. Finally, the U.S. under ex-US President Nixon preferred their own well-being. At least, Nixon thought so. A major problem in the U.S. is and has always been, a poor government and (extremely) rich and powerful corporations. In 1971 Anthony Sampson wrote *The Sovereign State*. He proved that multinationals make their own laws and set their own goals. Many Americans consider the Federal Government as disturbing, and their influence should be limited. The cradle of the free market trade doctrine that dominated the world economy over the past fifty years stood in America. In *Confessions of an Economic Hitman* John Perkins describes in detail how big U.S. based corporations have ruled the economies in the developing world after WWII, despite the Bretton Woods failure, and the declining power of the U.S. He named it 'corporatocracy'. Actually, the same names and families that form the financial elite are the ones behind this corporatocracy. Big money and big business go together as inseparable twins. The big U.S.-based corporations have used the IMF and World Bank to pursue their own goals. The big corporations were in fact all focused on gaining lots of money at the cost of the developing world. They could use both IMF and World Bank for their purposes, because from the start the U.S. had a decisive influence on the decision making processes within these institutes. One should read John Perkins' book to know how far the corporatocracy went to gain free access to the resources of the countries they were aiming at.

The corporatocracy holds U.S. politics in a firm grip. Their influence stretches so far, that they can make the military protect their interests.

The extremely violent air strike on Panama City on 20 December 1989 ordered by ex.-President George H.W. Bush (senior) causing many innocent victims is one of the many examples. The interests in the Panama Canal, and the foothold the U.S. had in South America appeared to have been the real reasons for this 'war'. In his movie *Fahrenheit 911* Michael Moore gives ample evidence of the bonded relations between politics, corporations, and military. For example, he shows how the U.S. Corporation Halliburton prospered from the Iraq war. This proves once more that the concepts of idealists such as the creation of the United Nations, IMF, and World Bank have been misused by the unlimited greedy. Therefore the idea of international cooperation and new world order gives me a taste of misleading people that hope for freedom and a better world.

Joseph Stiglitz, American, top economist and Nobel Prize winner blames the G20 leaders for with their policies creating precedents that have enlarged the probability of a new crisis. 'Most people are not aware that financial institutes were helped for years and years by their respective governments', he said in May 2010 in an interview with the Dutch newspaper *NRC*. 'As chief-economist with the World Bank I have experienced that in crisis situations dozens of times countries and their citizens did not benefit from bailouts, but the banks that had taken bad lending decisions, and had taken too much risk as well.' This happened in Argentina, Mexico, Russia, Thailand, Indonesia and many more countries. And because by means of deregulation we gave them the opportunity to do whatever they wanted, we may expect that it will happen again on short term'

Stiglitz is also very critical about the measures taken by President Obama. 'One of the core problems in the financial crisis was, that a number of financial institutes were 'too big to fail', and therefore simply could not go bankrupt. However, this policy did not apply for smaller financial institutions. They went bankrupt or were swallowed by their bigger competitors. Consequence of this policy is, that it just increased the problems instead of minimizing them. Financial institutions are still inclined to gamble and they still have the opportunity. If they win, the profit is theirs, if they lose the bill has to be paid by the taxpayer.'. If the Corporate Social Responsibility of banks is addressed, they present themselves as wolves in sheep's clothing. 'Greece has to learn discipline in their budget policy', according to the IMF, speaking on behalf of the international bankers.

The real interest of bankers is the same as that of any other Publicly Listed Corporation (PLC), and that is shareholder value. Making big money, without considering the social consequences. Without any moral objection banks such as Goldman Sachs and J.P.Morgan attacked the Greece state bonds, betting on a response of the government, and the movement of the euro. Attack smartly, invest sharply and the profit is always yours. This is what you might call the credo of those financial institutes that survived by means of the taxpayers money in many more countries than just the U.S. Banking and insurance corporation AIG received $ 180 billion support from the U.S. Government. This is the amount spent on foreign aid given to Africa over 25 years!

The impact of the global crisis on the Millennium Development Goals of the World Bank (September 2010)are as follows:

The global food, fuel and economic crises have set back progress to the MDGs (Milennium Devlopment Goals). An estimated 64 million more people are living on less than $1.25/day than there would have been without the crisis.

Weak demand in advanced economies, combined with more modest capital inflows and constrained ODA, has placed many developing countries under serious financial strain. Private capital flows to developing countries are forecast to recover from $454 billion (2.7 percent of GDP) in 2009 to $771 billion (3.2 percent of GDP) by 2012. As a result, the estimated external financing gap will halve to $180 billion from $352 billion in 2009. Increased borrowing by advanced countries, which already exceeded $2.5 trillion in 2009 (more than seven times the net capital flow to developing countries), could raise borrowing costs and crowd out developing country borrowers. Tighter financial conditions alone could lower growth in developing countries by up to 0.7 percentage points annually over the next five to seven years, and reduce potential output by up to 8 percent in the long run, compared with the pre-crisis trend.

Improvements in macroeconomic policies and progress on structural reforms in many developing countries generated greater resilience to economic shocks than in the past. But the global economic crisis has had a significant impact. While the impact has been varied among developing countries, growth fell from an average of about 7 percent in the five years preceding the crisis to 1.6 percent in 2009. The value of trade plunged by 12 percent in 2009 and – almost a year into the recovery – remains around 20 percent lower than its pre-crisis level; this is 40 percent lower than it would have been had world trade continued to grow at its 2002–08 trend rate.

Developing countries with fiscal space were able to at least partly offset the negative impact of the crisis with counter-cyclical macroeconomic policies backed by determined support from the international community. As a result, primary deficits in LICs increased significantly to an average of 2.1 percent of GDP in 2008-09 from an average of 0.58 percent of GDP over the previous five years. The ability of these countries to maintain spending in the face of a slow recovery is uncertain, as their stronger fiscal positions, ample reserves, and capacity to reprogram lower-priority spending have been eroded. While some emerging markets are regaining market access, others remain highly constrained and have had to finance about half of deficit increases domestically, mainly through bank borrowing and reserve draw downs. This has crowded out private-sector borrowing and raised sustainability concerns in a number of countries.

The crisis has slowed, and could potentially reverse, progress in attaining the MDGs. In 2010, an estimated 64 million more people will be living on less than $1.25 a day (76 million more on less than $2 a day) than would have been without the crises (table 1). Even by 2015, the number of additional poor people attributable to the global economic crisis is estimated to be 53 million (and 69 million based on $2 a day). The surge in food prices in 2008 drove an estimated 100 million more people into poverty.

SOURCE: WORLDBANK; UNFINISHED BUSINESS: MOBILIZING NEW EFFORTS TO ACHIEVE THE 2015 MILLENNIUM DEVELOPMENT GOALS SEPTEMBER 2010 (PAGES 12-14)

The set-back through the global crisis of the efforts to reduce hunger, illnesses, and deficiencies is enormous. The World Bank speaks of a 'challenge' to attain the goals set. The biggest problem is, that the richer countries in the World fail to donate sufficient funds. In the attempt to cut government expenses, the aid for developing countries comes generally first.

CHAPTER 6

BIS: the bankers' bank

When visiting Basel (Switzerland), at a five minutes' walk from the central station you come across the BIS Bank. The building has the shape of a large circular tower. Nothing outside it gives evidence of what is going on inside, just a modest plate on the wall next to the entrance, notifying in four languages that in the building the Bank for International Settlements is established. My question to people on a nearby terrace: 'What the building is used for?', remained unanswered. It is similar to the organization itself. As if it does not exist.

The Bank for International Settlements (BIS) was established in 1930 by bankers and diplomats of Europe and the United States. The shares of this bank were privately held. The initial goal of the bank was to collect and disburse Germany's World War I reparation payments. Although the BIS was organized as a commercial bank with privately owned shares, its immunity from government interference and taxes in both peace and war was guaranteed by an international treaty.

The BIS Bank soon evolved from war reparations organization to the position of bank of central bankers. Gold deposits and international transactions could safely be settled through the BIS Bank. As the world depression deepened in the 30th of the last century and the fear was great that the global financial system would collapse, there was a large need of a central point to coordinate the rescue efforts. The BIS Bank, established in a stable and well organized country, was the obvious meeting spot for international central bankers to discuss the future of finance.

The meeting spot was not only suitable for international bankers. In 'Big Business with Nazi Germany' 2009, historian Jacques Pauwels writes that U.S. captains of industry have financed Nazi Germany's war machine. The BIS Bank was the place to arrange the transfers of money. During the war the German Paul Hechler, member of the Nazi party was director of the BIS, and the American Thomas H. McKittrick [1] was chairman. Pauwels writes that: 'The BIS was the centre of a spiders' web of American bankers, business and lawyers and their Nazi German counterparts'.

> The B.I.S. continued its work during World War II as the medium through which the bankers — who apparently were not at war with each other — continued a mutually beneficial exchange of ideas, information, and planning for the post-war world. As one writer has observed, war made no difference to the international bankers:

The fact that the Bank possessed a truly international staff did, of course, present a highly anomalous situation in time of war. An American President was transacting the daily business of the Bank through a French General Manager, who had a German Assistant General Manager, while the Secretary-General was an Italian subject. Other nationals occupied other posts. These men were, of course, in daily personal contact with each other. Except for Mr. McKittrick they were of course situated permanently in Switzerland during this period and were not supposed to be subject to orders of their government at any time. However, the directors of the Bank remained, of course, in their respective countries and had no direct contact with the personnel of the Bank. It is alleged, however, that H. Schacht, president of the Reichsbank, kept a personal representative in Basle during most of this time.

It was such secret meetings, "... meetings more secret than any **ever** held by Royal Ark Masons or by any Rosicrucian Order..."between the central bankers at the "apex" of control that so intrigued contemporary journalists, although they only rarely and briefly penetrated behind the mask of secrecy.

WALL STREET AND THE RISE OF HITLER, 1976, BY ANTHONY SUTTON

The BIS contacts consisted amongst others of Nazi's and SS-officers in high places.... An SS officer that had excellent contacts with the BIS and the American Business partners', was Walter Schellenberg, head of infamous Sicherheitsdienst (SD) and staff member of Himmler. This organisation was specialized in collecting and cashing the stolen properties from the murdered Jews, and that of slave labourers in the camps. The money provided through the BIS Bank was used to feed the war machine with purchases outside Germany.

This quote gives further proof of the involvement of the BIS:

BIS Bank building Basel (Switzerland)

Indeed, exports did not begin to climb until the Germans, utilizing the Bank for International Settlements – BIS (*Bank für Internationalen Zahlungsausgleich - BIZ*), started to draw ever more frequently on gold and currency reserves seized in the occupied territories in order to pay for raw materials imported from the neutrals.

PORTUGAL AND THE NAZI GOLD, ANTONIO LOUÇA AND ANSGAR SCHÄFER

The Daily Bell, an Internet-based publication published on 28 August 2010 an article, written by Ron Holland, titled: **BIS: Trading With the Enemy - The Whole Story** (*http://www.thedailybell.com/1327/ BIS-Trading-With-the-Enemy-The-Whole-Story.html*). The Daily Bell has been developed by committed free-market thinkers who have been sharing their vision with the world in some cases since the late 1980s.

Ron Holland gives evidence of the role of the BIS and the international bankers and businesses before and during World War II. Here is a fragment:

"The BIS was a crucial facilitator, lending the laundering (of gold) an aura of honor among thieves. The BIS was a central transmission place where deals were struck, where the Portuguese representatives would meet the Reichsbank representatives," says Harold James, a Princeton University historian. And that's what kept money flowing into Nazi coffers.

In 1943, gasoline and petroleum products equaling the full capacity of the Spanish tanker fleet were traveling to Spain. From there, they were going directly to Germany. In addition to oil, sulfate of ammonia and cotton, both commodities in short supply in the U.S. were being shipped in huge amounts to Spain and from there on to Hitler.

The complete article is very worthwhile reading. The information is undeceiving and shocking, besides the role the Nazi's played, also the

American involvement though forbidden by the Congress is striking. Further, the fact that Basel was evacuated during WW II, and that it was so to speak a free place for international bankers and businessmen from the Nazi's as well as the Allies and neutral countries. It makes you remain perplexed on the fact that the BIS Bank has survived World War II.

After the war a big part of the stolen Nazi capital was deposited in countries such as Argentina as a pension fund for Nazi's who managed to get away. Of course, again, these transfers had been arranged by the BIS Bank. Also the war profits made in countries occupied by Germany by business men like William Rhodes Davis were transferred through the BIS Bank. Also millions of tons of iron ore used by the Nazi's to produce their tanks and artillery were purchased from Swedish companies trough intermediation of the BIS Bank. In 1944, following Czech accusations that the BIS was laundering gold that had been stolen from occupied Europe and murdered Jews, the American government backed a resolution at the Bretton Woods Conference calling for the liquidation of the BIS Bank.

The naïve idea was, that the international settlement and monetary-clearing functions it provided could be taken over by the newly established International Monetary Fund (IMF) and the World Bank. Seemingly in 1945 the role of the BIS was finished. In reality the bankers did not allow their club to be taken from them.

> After World War II, the BIS reemerged as the main clearing house for European currencies and, behind the scenes, the favored meeting place of central bankers. When the dollar came under attack in the 1960s, massive swaps of money and gold were arranged at the BIS for the defense of the American currency. It was undeniably ironic that, as the president of the BIS observed, "The United States, which had wanted to kill the BIS, suddenly finds it indispensable." In any case, the Fed has become a leading member of the club, with

either Chairman Paul Volcker or Governor Henry Wallich attending every "Basel weekend."'

SOURCE: 'RULING THE WORLD OF MONEY', BY EDWARD JAY EPSTEIN (1983)

As I said before, it is amazing how an organisation such as the BIS that has compromised itself to a great extent, could survive after the seriously questionable role they played before and during World War II. Apparently, the powers behind the BIS (remember it is (was) a privately owned bank) had that great influence that they managed to keep the bank alive. In the end history swiped away its role as intermediate between 'Wall Street' and Nazi Germany, the laundry of the stolen gold from by Nazi occupied countries and from Jews. Today, their role of bank of central bankers has been established in the world as I will show later in this chapter. Although the media speak of the Basel Committee, the Financial Stability Board, and when it comes to finance the IMF, it is obvious that the Bank for International Settlements is behind this all.

After World War II a democratizing process took place in the financial world. Central Banks were nationalized, governments became their owners. The United Nations were formed, and together with it for the international wellbeing the IMF and World Bank were established. The role of the BIS Bank remained indistinct during the first decades after WW II. The instruments to finance rebuilding the world economy were officially IMF and World Bank. However, behind the curtains the influence of the BIS Bank increased steadily.

In *Tragedy and Hope: A History of the World in Our Time* (1966), Dr. Carroll Quigley revealed the key role played in global finance by the BIS behind the scenes. Dr. Quigley was Professor of History at Georgetown University. He was also an insider, groomed by the powerful clique he called "the international bankers." His credibility is heightened by the fact that he actually espoused their goals.

He wrote:

> "I know of the operations of this network because I have studied it for twenty years and was permitted for two years, in the early 1960's, to examine its papers and secret records. I have no aversion to it or to most of its aims and have, for much of my life, been close to it and to many of its instruments. ....In general my chief difference of opinion is that it wishes to remain unknown, and I believe its role in history is significant enough to be known."

Quigley wrote of this international banking network:

> "The powers of financial capitalism had another far-reaching aim, nothing less than to create a world system of financial control in private hands able to dominate the political system of each country and the economy of the world as a whole. This system was to be controlled in a feudalist fashion by the central banks of the world acting in concert, by secret agreements arrived at in frequent private meetings and conferences. The apex of the system was to be the Bank for International Settlements in Basel, Switzerland, a private bank owned and controlled by the world's central banks which were themselves private corporations."

The key to their success, said Quigley, was that *'the international bankers would control and manipulate the money system of a nation while letting it appear to be controlled by the government'*. This statement echoes the role of the Rothschild's as described in chapter 4.

Carroll Quigly B.A., M.A., and Ph.D., was born in Boston, and attended Harvard University, where he studied history and earned B.A, M.A., and Ph.D. degrees. He taught at Princeton University, and then at Harvard, and then at the School of Foreign Service at Georgetown University from 1941 to 1976.

From 1941 until 1969, he taught a two-semester course at George-

town on the development of civilizations. According to the obituary in the Washington Star, many alumni of Georgetown's School of Foreign Service asserted that this was "the most influential course in their undergraduate careers".

In addition to his academic work, Quigley served as a consultant to the U.S. Department of Defense, the U.S. Navy, the Smithsonian Institution, and the House Select Committee on Astronautics and Space Exploration in the 1950s.

We may conclude that Carroll Quigly knew what he was talking about. His warnings against the aims of the financial elite, and the role of the Bank for International Settlements should have been taken very seriously. He simply was not allowed to speak about these things.

It is peculiar that the Bank for International Settlements has remained and still remains a dark horse for so long. Even now the BIS is referred to in the media as 'The Financial Stability Board' or 'The Basel Committee', and not as the bank of central bankers with an increasing powerful position. The currency that is issued by the BIS, the Special Drawing Rights, abbreviated as SDR is attributed to the IMF. However, the IMF is no more than an organization that executes financing programs, and does not issue money as the BIS actually does.

The BIS building in Basel, Switzerland attracts the attention of the visitor. It is a large circular tower that strikes the eye. The building is often compared with the Tower of Babel. It is said that what you can see is just a part of the complete premises. The processes that take place within this building are very non-transparent to an outsider. They have been compared with a Chinese Box.

In 1987 a 'Headquarters Agreement' was signed between the Swiss Federal Council and the BIS Bank. This agreement gave the BIS Bank a similar exceptional position as that of the Vatican. I mention a few fragments of the agreement to support this statement:

Article 3
Inviolability

1. The buildings or parts of buildings and surrounding land which, whoever may be the owner thereof, are used for the purposes of the Bank shall be inviolable. No agent of the Swiss public authorities may enter therein without the express consent of the Bank. Only the President, the General Manager of the Bank, or their duly authorised representative shall be competent to waive such inviolability.
2. The archives of the Bank and, in general, all documents and any data media belonging to the Bank or in its possession, shall be inviolable at all times and in all places.
3. The Bank shall exercise supervision of and police power over its premises.

Article 4
Immunity from jurisdiction and execution

The Bank shall enjoy immunity from jurisdiction, save:
(a) To the extent that such immunity is formally waived in individual cases by the President, the General Manager of the Bank, or their duly authorised representatives;
(b) In civil or commercial suits, arising from banking or financial transactions, initiated by contractual counterparties of the Bank, except in those cases in which provision for arbitration has been or shall have been made;
(c) In the case of any civil action against the Bank for damage caused by any vehicle belonging to or operated on behalf of the Bank.

Tax exemptions
The Bank, its assets, income and other property shall be exempt from direct Federal, cantonal and communal taxes. With regard to buildings, however, such exemption shall apply only to those owned by the Bank and occupied by its services, and to income deriving there from. The Bank shall not be subject to taxation on the rent it pays for premises rented by it and occupied by its services.

Immunity, inviolability, exercise supervision of and police power over its premises, tax exemptions, in a word: 'a state in the state'.

The BIS website informs us about the many activities as follows:

Banking activities financial services specifically designed to assist central banks and other official monetary institutions in the management of their foreign exchange reserves ,
The Basel Committee aims to improve risk management and governance as well as strengthen banks' transparency and disclosures The Committee's reforms are part of the global initiatives to strengthen the financial regulatory system that have been en-

dorsed by the **Financial Stability Board** (FSB) and the G20 Leaders.
Financial Stability Institute (FSI) to assist financial sector supervisors around the world in improving and strengthening their financial systems.

There are five more main activities and initiatives taken by the BIS; the above mentioned are the most important ones.

In contrast to the above six groups, the FSB has its own governance and reporting lines, as do the remaining two groups hosted at the BIS, the International Association of Deposit Insurers (IADI) and the International Association of Insurance Supervisors (IAIS).

The above listed activities emphasise the multitude of them. No wonder that the BIS organization has been compared with a Chinese Box. Also it gives an idea of not letting the right hand know what the left hand is doing.

Anyhow, though the BIS has the intent to be the bank for central bankers all over the world, from the website you get the idea that the BIS, and its related activities are merely a serving and consulting institute with no legislation power. However taking into account the volume of the financial transactions, and the influence their 'guidelines' Basel I and II have in the financial world one may say that they do not need legislation power. Remember the quote of Amschel Mayer Rothschild about the right to issue money:

"Let me issue and control a nation's money and I care not who writes the laws."

The assets of the BIS Bank had as per March 31 2010 a total value of SDR 258,893,300,000 or $ 392,262,575,800 of which a comparatively enormous amount of gold with a value in SDR of 43,039,800,000, which is *fourfold* the value of gold held by the FED.

The position of the BIS becomes clearer when contrasted to that of the U.S. Federal Reserve Bank. At the end of 2007 the central bank of the world's largest economy had under still more or less normal circumstances total assets amounting $915,129,000,000. One year later the total assets had been more than doubled, due to the massive issuing of dollars in order to fight the crisis.

The BIS made a *tax-free* profit in the year ending 31 March 2010 of **SDR 1,859,800,000**, which is in these troubled times a substantial result.

The question who presently owns the SDR 15.4 billion equity on the balance as per 31 March 2010 cannot be answered easily. According to unfounded information the 55 member central banks are owners of this equity. The former *private* shareholders have been 'compensated', so it says. *How* is completely unclear also who has been able to finance this massive buy-out. Yet at least it has been acknowledged that the BIS was in private hands for a longer period of time. What solution the private shareholders may have found to ensure their position is not clear. The register of shareholders is not open to the public. In other words, the BIS is not an Publicly Listed Company. This means that no outsider is able to verify the ownership of the BIS.

The board of the BIS consists of presidents of the main central banks from all over the world. At present (2010) this board consists of:

Christian Noyer, Paris
Chairman of the Board of Directors

Hans Tietmeyer, Frankfurt am Main
Vice-Chairman

Ben S Bernanke, Washington
Mark Carney, Ottawa

Mario Draghi, Rome
William C Dudley, New York
Philipp Hildebrand, Zurich
Stefan Ingves, Stockholm
Mervyn King, London
Jean-Pierre Landau, Paris
Henrique de Campos Meirelles, Brasília
Guy Quaden, Brussels
Fabrizio Saccomanni, Rome
Masaaki Shirakawa, Tokyo
Jean-Claude Trichet, Frankfurt am Main
Paul Tucker, London
Axel A Weber, Frankfurt am Main
Nout H E M Wellink, Amsterdam
Zhou Xiaochuan, Beijing

Striking is the fact that seated in this board are both Ben Bernanke (President of the FED Board) and William Dudley (President of the FED New York)

Zhou Xiaochuan, President of the Chinese Central Bank, and also a member of the BIS board, stated in an interview on 25 March 2009:

China wants yet to fulfill the vision that John Maynard Keynes had in 1944. President of the Chinese Central Bank Zhou Xiachuan pleads for introduction of the Bancor, an idea of the economist Keynes, proposed by him at the Bretton Woods conference and consequently rejected by the United States. The value of the Bancor would be based on thirty raw materials. China wants to replace the dollar for this currency as the new world reserve currency.

China is deeply concerned about the value of the dollar. To fight recession the U.S. government has issued a huge amount of new dollars. This may lead on the long run to mega inflation, and the collapse of the dollar. As China has invested 2 trillions of dollars in US treasury paper, this country is the largest creditor of the U.S. 'I call up the U.S. to keep their promise to take care for the Chinese assets, and to remain a trustworthy partner'.

Intentionally (?) he did not mention the SDR. To focus the attention on this currency might be too early. Generally the media deny plans in the direction of the SDR as the new world reserve currency.

The *Financial Times* missed the delicacy in the wordings of Zhao Xiachuan. The journalist mentioned in the following article written on 5 April 2009 not the Bancor but the SDR.

The SDR as new world reserve currency is according to the FT unlikely:

G20 pledge on SDRs unlikely to threaten dollar

One of the more surprising elements in the package assembled by the G20 was the decision to create $250bn in special drawing rights, a form of basket "currency" used by the International Monetary Fund. On top of the pledge to increase the IMF's resources by the Group of 20 leading and emerging nations, the creation of SDRs – the first such decision since 1981 – might be regarded by some as a further shift towards global economic management of liquidity and the financial system.

The issue was given more prominence when a recent paper by Zhou Xiaochuan, governor of the People's Bank of China, the Chinese central bank, mooted the idea of the SDR supplanting the dollar as a global reserve currency – together with a widely misunderstood remark by Tim Geithner, US Treasury secretary, who welcomed the SDR allocation but not ending the dollar's reserve currency role. Indeed, experts say a single creation of SDRs is a long way from a fundamental remaking of the worldwide economic order. Nor will it make the IMF itself bigger or more powerful. As the IMF says: "The SDR is neither a currency, nor a claim on the IMF."

The SDR is not much more than an accounting unit used between governments and the IMF, made up of a basket of four widely-traded currencies – the dollar, the euro, sterling and the yen. One SDR is worth about £1, so a dollar buys 0.67 SDRs. SDRs are counted as part of government reserves and may be used as collateral for borrowing, meaning that their creation in effect can mean increasing the global money supply.

The $250bn (€185.4bn, £169bn) in SDRs will go not to the IMF but to the member governments, according to their "quotas" or contributions to the fund. Since the larger quotas are held by richer countries, they must give or lend shares to poorer countries to achieve the aim of helping emerging market governments struggling with a loss of confidence and liquidity. But since SDRs are an aggregation of existing currencies, creating more will not automatically supplant the dollar. Brad Setser of the Council on Foreign Relations points out: "If China wants to diversify its reserves out of the dollar, it can do so right now. There is nothing to stop a country like Brazil issuing debt denominated in SDRs and nothing to stop China buying them."

Some experts think China wants to redenominate some of its huge dollar holdings into SDRs without selling dollars on the open market – which would risk a crash in the US currency and a fall in the value of its reserves. But they say the US and the other countries whose currencies make up the SDR are unlikely to agree.

The arguments that are brought forward to trifle a possible future role for the SDR as global reserve currency are at least naïve. Maybe there is no awareness of the increasing power of the BIS. However, this seems rather unlikely. In this context I remind the reader of the role the ECU played before the euro was introduced on 1 January 2002. The ECU was just like the SDR nowadays not a currency, but certainly a forerunner of the euro. The fact that the journalist did not adopt the Bancor as the currency Zhao Xiachuan talked about but the SDR seems awkward. It might also have been a way of taking the opportunity to make short shrift with any speculation about the role of the SDR and the new world order once and for all.

The fact that US Treasury Secretary and former President of the FED New York, Geithner, strongly opposed the idea of the Bancor is also striking. Later this was denied. 'His words were explained wrongly'. Undoubtedly the US are not willing to give up the position of the dollar as world reserve currency that easily. I have made clear that although there were some disadvantages, the position of the dollar has brought the U.S. and especially the big corporations many financial returns. Furthermore the program of injecting massive amounts of dollars in the US economy, especially in the financial sector was not ready yet. Losing the position of world reserve currency would have speeded up the crash of the dollar.

Incidentally the massive dollar input has made the rich even richer and the poor still poorer. This example shows how it works: The financial crisis has lead to massive write offs of receivables on the bank balances. 70% of their original value was often taken as a loss. The trade in the financial products mentioned in Chapter 1 was more or less dead. In order to revitalise this trade the U.S. government subsidises the *healthy investors* such as Goldman Sachs, J.P. Morgan, etc. to buy the financial products from troubled banks. The intended result was that banks had again money available and would be back in business. Subsidising this took the U.S. government one trillion of dollars. And the winners of this game were... the healthy investors! The receivables had in reality a higher value than according to their book value. Once the market started to move again the buyers could consequently sell the 'products' at a higher price, earn a lot and also receive the promised government subsidy. The shareholders of Goldman Sachs, J.P.Morgan etc. were pleased, and the bank managers earned again big bonuses. However, the one trillion dollars are a cheque, drawn on the American people, that has to be paid back in future by raising taxes, and through inflation. Inflation is a decline of the value of money. One can buy less with the same dollar. Inflation has a clear advantage for debtors, especially when the debtor is a government. Through inflation prices and wages and therefore value added taxes and wage taxes tend to increase. For the same amount of debt governments have more money available to make down payments and pay interest.

Now let's return to the activities of the Bank for International Settlements and especially the coordination of the international monetary policy. The Basel Committee (= BIS organisation) is the founding father of the Basel I, Basel II and Basel III agreements. The Basel II agreement dating back to 2005 has been designed to set requirements for the minimum amount of guaranteed capital of commercial banks. Compliance to this agreement means, that banks need to have at least 8 euros guaranteed capital on each 92 euros lent out.

Guaranteed capital means that this capital is available to serve as a buffer for possible losses. The agreements have more far-reaching consequences than just this requirement. They also stipulate the way to handle risk perceived by businesses. Each business client of any commercial bank has a risk-profile. This risk-profile determinates whether the company is creditworthy or not. Also the conditions at which money can be borrowed are strictly formulated in the Basel agreements.

The requirements are so strict that it will be, and actually is by now, very hard for Small and Medium Sized Enterprises (SMEs) to meet them. Due to the financial crisis commercial banks in countries all over the world have become very, if not extremely, cautious and more than ever before inclined to comply to the Basel Agreements. In their computer systems, most of the banks have already included the Basel directives. The lending process has become completely computerized. The account managers of banks have no authority whatsoever anymore to make their own decisions. It is the computer that determines. Red is forget it. Green is agreed. Even more, autumn 2010, the Basel III agreement will be accepted by the G20, and banks have to strengthen their capital buffers. The target capital that has to be reached by 2019 will make banks even more risk-avoiding. SMEs will have a very hard time to have access to bank credit.

SMEs are victims of this new policy, although they were certainly not the cause of the financial crisis, as pointed out in chapter 1. In the media in U.K., Germany, The Netherlands regularly news articles appear about the extreme restrictive attitude of banks towards SMEs. Realizing the important role SMEs play in regional economies, particularly employment and also the social cohesion of a region, the conclusion must be that Basel I and II and in the near future Basel III are no good news for the SMEs, and neither for a country's economy.

Governments are willing to help the SMEs with their financing problems. However, their options are very limited now the financial institutes have placed governments in a heavy debt position. The cynical truth is thus that banks are not willing to finance SMEs, and those same banks are the cause of the big government debts, preventing them to help SMEs effectively.

Recent facts indicate that the governmental efforts in the U.S. to revitalize the economy begin to miss their desired effect. In other countries, such as U.K., France, Italy, The Netherlands etc. the same is likely to happen. The U.S. is just a step ahead because they started earlier with the massive injection of dollars in the economy. The status quo is likely to return. Combined with a massive government debt this can only lead to more trouble, more unemployment, more bankruptcies of both businesses and private persons, dissatisfaction, social unrest etc.

Here are just two letters out of the many more from common British people that depict clearly the present situation, and makes us fear for what lies ahead:

Pay rose by 1.9% over the last year, well below the current consumer price inflation rate of 3.4% and retail price inflation of 5.1%. The figure for pay including bonus payments jumped by 4.2%, showing how banks and other financial institutions felt able to pay top up payments to staff.' I just heard this on the BBC and couldn't believe it. Who are these monkeys surveying, I neither got 1.9% and do not get a bonus.

If the government uses the 4.2% as an average pay rise to impose new taxes and fix the figures I will be £^$%ed by at least 3% on top of inflation, surely along with most other people? I don't believe anything these liars are putting out, inflation is higher than they are regularly reporting and pay rises 75% lower. How much of the unemployment figures are a lie to make sure it stays below 2.5m as long as possible? My god, how bad really is it that they are hiding as much as possible based on these 'statistics'?

The more important figure is the number of economically inactive now 8.21m or 21 per cent of the population. I don't give any credibility to the current unemployment figures it is more than 7.9 per cent of the population claiming, they exclude a whole raft of people when it suits the state as being unemployed. Cut, cut,cut,cut, cut and cut again. Thee British seem so masochistic, like, we've had a good time and now we have to pay. Well, listen up, you're not paying for the good time you've had you're paying, and you're going to keep paying, to cover the costs of bailing out your rich neighbours working in the City. These neighbours of yours get annual bonuses that would make you weep - even a small(ish) bonus trumps what most people EARN in a year!

SO, whine a little, and take your medicine. It's gonna take lots of cuts, cuts, cuts to cover the banking bailout black hole. See you down the job centre.

SOURCE: THE GUARDIAN, FINANCIAL CRISIS FORUM 2010

The developments in Europe and North America will be good news for those who have a new world order in mind with one world currency and one central bank, controlling the worldwide monetary system. Conspiracy theory? I think not. Read what Ben Bernanke said in a speech for the Council of Foreign Affairs:

Bernanke To CFR: New Financial Authority Is Needed

"Reform of financial regulation and supervision should be coordinated internationally to the greatest extent possible." Federal Reserve Chairman Ben Bernanke has told an elite gathering that a new overarching financial authority should be created by the government and empowered with sweeping new regulatory responsibilities.

"We must have a strategy that regulates the financial system as a whole, in a holistic way, not just its individual components," Bernanke said in a speech to the Council on Foreign Relations. "From the perspective of the G20, the focus should be on the international aspects, obviously, of this crisis. I talked today primarily of what the United States can do and I left implicit, perhaps I shouldn't have in front of the Council On Foreign Relations, the fact that this is very much an international problem, and it requires international solutions. We need to begin to establish a framework... The better goal for a meeting of leaders would be as much as possible to establish some principles that would guide reforms around the world... they need to work for institutions and for markets that cross borders. We have banks and insurance companies that have subsidiaries in 100 or 120 countries, and there are so many jurisdictions, that dealing with problems in one of those companies is extraordinarily complicated. In order to do that successfully, we need to have agreements, conventions, that will help us work across jurisdictions in an effective and cooperative way."

SOURCE: STEVE WATSON , TUESDAY, MARCH 10, 2009

Reading between the lines makes it crystal clear that the thoughts of this chief player in the monetary system is in the direction of one bank, one currency, setting aside democracy all over the world.

A supranational bank, not under the control of any democratically chosen parliament makes me hesitant of what lies ahead of us if this bank is the sole centre of a new worldwide monetary system.

In a speech on the future mandate of the 186-nation Washington-based lending organization on 26 February 2010, IMF Head Dominique Strauss Kahn referred to the future role on the SDR. This speech has been generally ignored by the mainstream media.

Dominique Strauss-Kahn, the head of the International Monetary Fund, suggested Friday the organization might one day be called on to provide countries with a global reserve currency that would serve as an alternative to the U.S. dollar. "That day has not yet come, but I think it is intellectually healthy to explore these kinds of ideas now," he said in a speech on the future mandate of the 186-nation Washington-based lending organization.

Strauss-Kahn said such an asset could be similar to but distinctly different from the IMF's special drawing rights, or SDRs, the accounting unit that countries use to hold funds within the IMF. It is based on a basket of major currencies.

SOURCE: HTTP://MAXKEISER.COM/2010/02/27/HEAD-OF-IMF-PROPOSES-NEW-GLOBAL-CURRENCY

¹) T.H. MCKITTRICK AND THE BIS

U.S. citizen Thomas Harrington McKittrick, in 1939, was made president of the Bank for International Settlements whose originally stated purpose was to provide the Allies with reparations to be paid by Germany for World War I. McKittrick's offsiders were Hermann Schmitz, head of I.G. Farben, Baron Kurt von Schroder, head of the J.H. Stein Bank of Cologne [officer and financier of the Gestapo], Dr. Walther Funk of the Reichsbank and Emil Puhl. Funk and Puhl were Hitler's personal appointees to the board.

In March 1938, when the Nazis marched into Vienna, much of the gold of Austria was looted and packed into vaults controlled by the Bank for International Settlements. Later, at the Nuremberg trials, Funk said that Puhl had informed him in 1942 that the Gestapo had deposited gold coins, and other gold, from the concentration camps, in the Reichsbank. Puhl had been in charge of this. Jewels, monocles, spectacle frames, watches, cigarette cases, and gold dentures had flowed into the Reichsbank, supplied by Puhl from Heinrich Himmler's resources. They were melted down into gold bars; he did not add how many bars were marked for shipment to Switzerland. Each gold bar weighed 20 kilograms.

In March 1939, storm troopers arrested the directors of the Czech National Bank and demanded that they yield up $48 million gold reserve. The Czechs said that they had already shifted the gold to the BIS with instructions that it be forwarded to Montagu Norman at the Bank of England. The Czech directors asked the Dutch BIS president, J.W. Beyen, to return the gold to Basel. Beyen spoke with BIS general manager Roger Auboin of the Bank of France, then called London and instructed Norman to return the gold, which Norman did and the gold went to fund Germany's war effort. Or did it? J.W. Beyen ran into London economic journalist Paul Einzig who asked about the Czech gold, to which Beyen replied: "It is all technical. The gold never left London."

The arrangement between the BIS and its member banks was that transactions were not normally made by shipments, as that would show up in counts. Thus, Montagu Norman authorized Beyen and then replaced the same amount from the Czech National Bank holdings in London. Sir Otto Niemeyer of the Bank of England, BIS board member and Chairman Montague Norman remained in office for the BIS throughout the war. On May 27, 1941, Secretary of State Cordell Hull telegraphed U.S. Ambassador John G. Winant in London, asking for a report on the continuing relationship between the BIS and the British government. Niemeyer admitted that the government of Great Britain was still a client of the Bank and had accepted a dividend from it, largely from Nazi sources. Niemeyer said that he believed the British should continue the association for the duration as well as lend the Bank their tacit approval, "If only for the reason that a useful role in post-war settlements might later have an effect."

Just after February 5, 1942, McKittrick was reappointed and arranged a loan of several million Swiss gold francs to the Nazi government of Poland and the collaborative government of Hungary. In the spring of 1943, he was issued an Italian diplomatic visa to travel by train and auto to Rome and was met at the border by the SS, who gave him safe conduct. McKittrick then went to Lisbon and by Swedish ship to the United States. In Manhattan in April he had meetings with Leon Fraser and with the heads of the Federal Reserve Bank. He then went to Berlin on a U.S. passport to provide Emil Puhl of the Reichsbank with intelligence on financial problems and high-level attitudes in the United States.

At Bretton Woods, in 1944, it was proposed that the BIS be dissolved. Bankers Winthrop Aldrich an Edward E. (Ned) Brown of the American delegation and the Chase and First National banks, the Dutch delegation, J.W. Beyen, Leon Fraser of the First National Bank of New York and the British delegation, supported by Anthony Eden and the Foreign Office, strongly opposed the dissolution. John Maynard

Keynes pleaded with the proposers that the BIS remain intact. After the war, McKittrick was given a post by the Rockefellers and Winthrop Aldrich: vice-president of the Chase National Bank, a position he occupied for several years. In 1950 he invited Emil Puhl to the United States as his honoured guest.

source: *The World is in Good Hands*, James Higham, 2010

CHAPTER 7

Financial and Economic Crisis

The recession that hit the World in 2007 began with a financial crisis. The causes of this financial crisis have been explained in Chapter 1 above. Yet the question why a financial crisis should be followed by an economic crisis remains unanswered. Besides, the concepts financial and economic crisis are often jumbled up. So what is the connection between the two?

Simply put it is the money that connects the monetary and economic systems. Why is it that money plays such a crucial and dominant role? The answer on this question is to be found in the banking system. There is a mechanism that enables bankers to increase and to contract the money supply. If the money supply is ample economic activities are promoted. However, if the money supply contracts economic activities will be discouraged. Economic activities are thus dependent on the money supply. Research on the development of money supply, Gross Domestic Product (GDP), and income over the years 1990 – 2006 in the Netherlands (source CBS), shows that the GDP (the value of all that the economy produces in goods and services in a certain country

in a year) more than doubled over that period. Income (from wages and salaries) also increased but less than the GDP. This means that employees did not fully benefit from the higher GDP. However, the development of the money supply increased amazingly to nearly sevenfold of what it was in 1990. This teaches us a number of things:
- Firstly, that in times of economic growth, the money supply increases. However, this is not necessary in line with the growth of the GDP.
- Secondly, that employees do not always get the full – relative – benefits of an increasing GDP, because the wages and salaries might not hold pace with the growing GDP.

Where does all this money not justified by the growth of the GDP go to? Part of it might be explained by investments. Before the return on investment is earned there is the expenditure for the investment itself. However, theoretically, an investment would lead to the same increase in both money supply and GDP. For example, if one buys a new house and borrows the full amount to finance this, the money supply increases. At the same time the builder earns the same amount by building the house for the contracted price. So, these two activities, borrowing money and building a house, will lead to the same increase in money supply and in GDP. The only sensible conclusion that can be drawn from this, is that a lot of money has been issued that did not lead to an equally higher GDP, and neither to more private wealth of those who have their income from wages and salaries. Who says common people have lived a too luxurious life in recent years?

In the euro zone the money supply increased during the years 2002-2009 at 75%, whilst the GDP grew with no more than 10%. So, the phenomenon I have depicted above is not typically Dutch. In times of economic recession the money supply contracts. During the great depression in the thirties of the last century the money supply decreased by one-third. This number is the outcome of a research done by the economist Milton Friedman (*Capitalism and Freedom*).

In the case of this crisis there is essentially no difference. The money supply has a tendency to contract in the U.S. as well as in Europe. That it remains more or less on the same level, is due to the massive injections of currencies by the respective governments. For disciples of the monetary economic theory this is blasphemy. The idea is that by contracting the money supply the economy cools down, and will regain stability on a lower level. That this goes together with a lot of human misery (e.g. unemployment, loss of property, poverty) is not the primary concern of these economists. It is the system that is sacred, because in their opinion it is nature's way. Seven fat years, seven meager years.

Is the 'solution' chosen by the U.S., the euro zone countries, U.K., Japan, etc. the right one? I don't think so. It is no more than postponing the inevitable moment that debts have to be cut back. Now already Greece, Iceland, Spain, Portugal, Italy, Ireland are deeply in trouble. More countries will follow if the present policies of 'keep the economy going and hope that the economy will find its way up again' have lost their effect. The European research institute LEAP/E2020 [2] compares

the approach of the governments of countries to their troubled economies with the treatment of people who are suffering from a grave disease, with no prospect on recovery. As long as the system remains unchanged, crises will occur. It is inherent in it. Countries, businesses, and
private households are heavily in debt. Debt that has been created during times of booming economy. Due to the crisis, debt has become a too
heavy burden. People, businesses and countries are not able to repay
their debts. Large numbers of private and business bankruptcies, and
countries in trouble are the consequences of this. And the rich? Well,
this is what Thomas Jefferson, third President of the U.S. said about it:

> 'If the American people ever allow private banks to control the issue
> of currency... the banks and corporations that will grow up around
> them will deprive the people of their property until their children
> wake up homeless on the continent their fathers conquered.'

Banks and corporations. Yes, but in that sense that they are merely
the instruments of the financial elite. The cynical part is, that they
'harvest' the properties of people during times of crisis. First countries,
businesses, and private households are flooded with money (as debt)
during times of a booming economy . This money has been created out
of thin air, so strictly spoken no man owns it, neither does the financial
elite. Consequently, man is deprived from his property during times of
a downturn in the economy because being unable to repay the debts
the property is appropriated by the banks. *The only reason why this
can happen over and over again, is because we collectively have come
to believe that money has value in itself.*

Money has no value, no more than being a medium of exchange. Neither is money a product. The real value can be found in what we produce in goods and services. People, working together in a business or
organization create a value chain. The only real purpose of money is to
make things possible, and to support the creation and maintenance of
these value chains. If we point an accusing finger at the financial elite,

we should be aware that we are the ones that have collectively believed in this monetary system, as if it were 'God-made', and therefore allowed it to be what it has become.

In Chapter 5 I have explained that due to the crisis the position of small and medium sized enterprises (SMEs) is under pressure. Our present monetary system is rather hostile to SMEs. In 2009 a report was published by the Organization for Economic Co-operation and Development (OECD) titled 'SMEs and Global Crisis'. This report underlines the important role SMEs play in the economies of countries all over the world. At the same time the OECD explains why SMEs have a hard time nowadays to borrow the money needed to finance, and expand the business. Let alone the money needed for innovation.

Importance of SMEs in "normal times" and in times of crisis

SMEs and entrepreneurs play a significant role in all economies and are the key generators of employment and income, and drivers of innovation and growth. In the OECD area, SMEs employ more than half of the labour force in the private sector. In the European Union, they account for over 99 % of all enterprises. Furthermore, 91 % of these enterprises are micro-firms with less than 10 workers. Given their importance in all economies, they are essential for the economic recovery. Even in 'normal' economic conditions governments have recognised that, to survive and grow, SMEs need specific policies and programmes – hence the comprehensive range of SME measures currently in place across the OECD members. However, at the present time, SMEs have been especially hard hit by the global crisis. These firms are more vulnerable now for many reasons: not only has the traditional challenge of accessing finance continued to apply, but new, particularly supply-side, difficulties are currently apparent. It is important to stress that SMEs are generally more vulnerable in times of crisis for many reasons among which are:
• it is more difficult for them to downsize as they are already small;

- they are individually less diversified in their economic activities;
- they have a weaker financial structure (i.e. lower capitalisation);
- they have a lower or no credit rating;
- they are heavily dependent on credit and
- they have fewer financing options.

SMEs in global value chains are even more vulnerable as they often bear the brunt of the difficulties of the large firms.

Impact of the global crisis on SME and entrepreneurship financing
Although there is no internationally agreed definition of small and medium sized enterprises (SMEs), the evidence suggests that these firms are being affected by the financial and economic crisis across economies. There is evidence that SMEs in most countries are confronted with a clear downturn in demand for goods and services if not a demand slump in the fourth quarter of 2008. Many expect a further worsening to come. For SMEs there are two related stress factors:

a) increased payment delays on receivables which added - together with an increase in inventories- result in an endemic shortage of working capital and a decrease in liquidity and

b) an increase in reported defaults, insolvencies and bankruptcies.

© OECD 2009

The above section of the OECD report makes clear that SMEs can be considered the backbone of a country's economy. Above all, SMEs often are the main suppliers of employment. SME's employ more than half of the labour force in the private sector of countries in the European Union. In this crisis the vulnerability of SMEs comes forward in the development of sales, liquidity problems, and the restrictive attitude of banks. A consequence of this is that many SME's have to lay off employees and worse, go bankrupt. An increasing number of SMEs have gone bankrupt. For example, the Dutch bankruptcies register shows an increase of 24% in 2010 compared to 2009. In the U.S. business bankruptcies have risen from 30,741 in 2007 to 49,091 in 2008, and 61,148 in 2009. For the correct interpretation of these numbers one should consider that business bankruptcies in the U.S. are often prevented by some form of debt agreement. Not only for-profit SMEs also not-for-profit SMEs, like museums and theatres are victims of the crisis. For example in Germany:

> A study released Wednesday claims that every 10th museum or cultural institution in Germany may be forced to close by 2020 due to lack of funds. The report was released by management consulting firm A.T. Kearney. Around 8 billion euros ($10.2 billion) in public funds are given each year to German cultural institutions, and the study's authors expect an eight to 10 percent drop in that number by 2020. The report also claims that museum operating costs will increase by 24 percent over the same period.
> "Due to the financial crisis, cities and counties have to invest their money elsewhere and not in culture. We expect to see this trend continue over the next decade," Claudia Witzemann, head author of the study, told Deutsche Welle.

SOURCE: HTTP://WWW.DW-WORLD.DE 19 AUGUST 2010

Also employment is becoming more and more of a problem in Europe and North America. The unemployment figures suggest a reasonably stable situation. Nevertheless, the number of jobs available in the private sector especially SMEs, and qualified jobs have dropped dramatically, in The Netherlands by more than 500,000 as from 2007 until 2010. Again I will use the opinion of readers of The Guardian, this time about the unemployment/employment situation in the UK to make clear how bad things are, also in that country:

> Re: article dated 14th July 2010 that indicates unemployment figures have recently fallen (& the corresponding statistics to 'prove' this claim). Given that it is summer it is hardly surprising that un-

employment has fallen slightly. Having worked for the Dept for Work & Pensions for 20 years I am aware that seasonal jobs in the tourist sectors, catering & hospitality swallow up a proportion of the unemployed. In northern seaside towns like Blackpool jobs are a plenty in the summer season, compared to winter. However, when autumn comes around just watch the figures rise again as temporary, seasonal work ceasing. The government's recent statistics might look good on paper, but not only are many of the available jobs part time, they are also temporary. Additionally, they are not necessarily the jobs that make long term careers, but rather 'fillers' for the hundreds of university graduates who find themselves 'frying burgers' to pay off their student loans, instead of the careers which they had hoped a university education might offer them. (There is nothing wrong with frying burgers, by the way, but such positions are not going to pay the student loan off so quickly, or in the long term pay a mortgage & support a family). Don't be fooled by statistics which show a drop in unemployment figures. The government congratulate itself on falling unemployment figures when the majority have been given the opportunity to do meaningful work which offers job security & pays the bills!

Employment lags economic recovery by some distance, since the economy has barely scraped from recession and its growth is at best extremely low, how is it possible that there is a record drop in the claimant count?

I would suggest the record drop is not because these people have found work, but simply have dropped from claiming the dole or have moved to training. Even the States which exited from recession long before the UK is still suffering job losses but somehow in the UK we have managed to create some kind of a miracle of employment?

There are, and always have been, two Britains that somehow co-exist. In Feelgood Britain people still have jobs, still have careers, and are feeling really quite good about the substantial reductions in their mortgage repayments.

In Non-Feelgood Britain, the part that the Labour party was meant
to care for and support, people who, for the most part, are used to
living near to or below the poverty line on low wages or no wages,
life has become even harder, and in some cases intolerable - due
to greater unemployment; reduced working hours, reduced wages
and reduced opportunities; inflation, higher rents, etc.

SOURCE: *THE GUARDIAN*, UNEMPLOYMENT FORUM DISCUSSION 2010

In August 2010 youth unemployment reached 567,000 in the U.K.
The universities tend to be overcrowded as more and more students
extend their education rather than seek employment. This is a time
where again as in the thirties of the 20th century academics and high-
ly-trained professionals have no other choice than frying hamburgers
to earn a (very modest) living, pay their expensive mortgages, and pay

off their student loans. Simply because there are a limited amount of qualified jobs available. In The Netherlands, and presumably also in other European countries, a way has been found to pimp the unemployment statistics up. Some 900,000, mainly young people became so-called Self-Employed Entrepreneurs Without Employees (ZZPers), which actually means that they have a business but, for the greater part, (virtually) no work.

SMEs that could play an important role in the supply of new and especially qualified jobs, are not in the position to do so. Who will stand up for the SMEs? Apparently not the banks. I will come back on that subject. The OECD feels responsibility for SMEs. Again a fragment from the report 'Impact of the Global Crisis on SMEs':

> The OECD Working Party on SMEs and Entrepreneurship (WPSMEE), in close cooperation with its parent Committee, the CIIE:
> - Could promote a Scoreboard on SME and entrepreneurship financing data and policies (a pilot project will be carried out in the framework of the 2009-2010 programme of work in view of the "Bologna +10" High level Meeting); and
> - Should monitor, report on, and discuss SME and entrepreneurship financing trends on a regular basis.
> - As a follow-up, the WPSMEE should also carry out, in the framework of its programme of work 2009-2010, an assessment of the effectiveness of measures taken to assist SMEs and entrepreneurs in weathering the financial and economic crisis, as reported in the present report.
> - Finally, the OECD should also continue facilitating the Tripartite Dialogue between governments, SMEs and the financial institutions, to periodically review progress in strengthening SME and entrepreneurship financing.

The OECD wants to promote the discussion between governments, SMEs and financial institutions, for they need to monitor, and report on the developments around SMEs. More they cannot do. The OECD has no financial power like the BIS Bank has. The Tripartite Dialogue until so far has not had any real impact. Bankers say that the loans to SMEs are at a normal level, and that it is quite clear that in times of crisis 'things happen'. Governments try to find solutions that do not cost them too much money or increase the risk of having to pay for business failures in the future. And the SMEs and their representatives like in the Netherlands 'MKB Nederland' keep on reporting about the many businesses that are in deep trouble, and about the often harsh and selfish attitude of banks towards SMEs. In the end the stories are trifled as 'nagging'. And the status quo remains.

Banks have never considered SMEs as their core business. It is not where the 'big money' can be made. Furthermore, banks do not see the need to consider themselves socially responsible. Their main goal is to create shareholder value. The basis for this is the above mentioned *fractional banking*. With a relatively very low amount of equity (owned by the shareholders), banks lend out money nine times or more as what the shareholders have paid-in. Take, for example, a starting bank. This bank has fulfilled all legal requirements and received a banking license. The shareholder has paid in $ 1 million. Does the banker have to wait for savers before he can lend out money? No, he is allowed to create new money. The only thing the banker needs is a signature under the loan contract from the borrower. During the first year of its existence the bank lends out $ 9 million (created out of thin air) at an interest of 10%. Interest income therefore is $ 900,000. Operational expenses are $ 400,000. Net income (ignoring taxes) is then $ 500,000. The return on investment for this new banker is $ 500,000/$ 1 million = 50%!

This is how fractional banking works. The most important goal for the young banker is to find the 'good risks'. That is, finding lenders that pay a fine amount of interest, and at the same time carry a low amount of risk. Therefore, commercial banks will be inclined to do acquisition on well-established, bigger companies. SMEs are not in their core potential client group. It must be really annoying for banks that governments push to give loans to SMEs. Reluctant as they are, in many cases banks are only willing to consider this if governments grant subsidies and guarantees. Back to the example. The new banker has lent out the total amount of $900,000 to SMEs. Suddenly there is the CRISIS. 50% of the businesses go bankrupt. This means a loss of $450,000, and a big impact on profitability. His own capital has been reduced to almost half of what he paid in. This shows clearly why solid bankers are risk averse, and also why they are generally spoken not pleased with a too big part of SMEs in their portfolios. And what about savings? Banks do have savings from private persons, organisations, and businesses. Banks do not really care for them either. They are a source of available capital. If someone puts $ 1 million savings on the bank, there is a basis for lending out another $ 9 million, again created out of thin air. But giving guarantees that the savings will be paid back under all circumstances? No, that is –again- not the bank's responsibility.

Recently the Basel Committee (BIS) stated as follows:

> The Basel Committee is designing 'resolution schemes'. Central banks will be allowed in the future to disown banks. Shareholders will be set aside, and creditors have to accept losses.

Who are a bank's creditors? Amongst others, they are the savers. In other words, banks treat savers as if they were the owners of a bank without giving them the privileges and the returns that shareholders receive. If it had not been a serious report, produced by serious and experienced men, one would be inclined to laugh about it. What was one of the main conclusions in a report on The Future of Banks, issued on 7 April 2009 in The Netherlands? 'Banks should direct themselves primarily to savers (private and business). Savers have paid in more (debt) capital in banks than shareholders.' The observation, made in the same report that banks have a *public utility function* is also a good one… Banks should have a public utility function, but they do not because it is not their mission.

Of course nothing has changed since the issue of the report. Almost all commercial banks would not want savers to interfere with their business. Neither do they see themselves as serving a public goal. The conclusion is, that banks in their present form are unable to serve social economic goals. They are simply not made for this. Therefore, reform of the banking system is not enough.

The only real solution would be:
- ending fractional reserve banking,
- ending shareholder value as the basis for banking activities, and
- not allowing banks to issue money out of thin air.

In the days of Benjamin Franklin and the Colonial Script, governments should issue debt-free money themselves. Enough to support a healthy economic development, with money in a purely subservient function.

This would truly open the door for SMEs especially those that contribute to a sustainable, and environmentally friendly economy.

Research institute LEAP [1] published in 2010 an article that makes the influence of the monetary system on the economy quite clear:

Where the real big money is.....Goldman Sachs' role in this Greek tragedy... and the next sovereign defaults:
In the « Greek case », just like in every suspense story, a « bad guy » is needed. In this phase of the global systemic crisis, the role of the « bad guy » is usually played by one of Wall Street's big investment banks, in particular by the leader of the gang, Goldman Sachs. The « Greek case » is no different. This New York investment bank is directly involved in the budgetary conjuring tricks which allowed Greece to qualify for Euro entry, whilst its actual budget deficits would have disqualified it. In reality it was Goldman Sachs who, in 2002, created one of its cunning financial models of which it holds the secret and which, almost systematically resurfaces several years later, to blow up the client. But what does it matter, since GS (Goldman Sachs) profits were the beneficiary!

In the Greek case what the investment bank proposed was very simple: raise a loan which didn't appear in the budget a swap agreement(1) which enabled a ficticious reduction in the size of the Greek public deficit. The Greek leaders at the time were, of course, 100% liable and should be subjected to Greek and European political and legal process for having cheated the EU and their own citizens within the framework of a major historic event, the creation of the single European currency. But, let's be clear, the liability of the New York investment bank (as an accomplice) is just as great, even greater perhaps because Goldman Sachs was well aware of what tricks they played.

Considering the importance of Goldman Sachs in world financial affairs these last few years, nothing that this bank does should leave governments and legislators indifferent. It is Paul Volcker, current head of Barack Obama's financial advisors, who has become one of the strongest critics of Goldman Sachs' activities. We already had the occasion to write, at the time of the election of the current US President, that he is the only person in his entourage having the experience and skills to push through tough measures and who, at this moment, knows what, or rather whom, he is talking about. With this same logic, on the issue of transparency in financial activities and state budgets and using the ill-fated role of Goldman Sachs and of the large investment banks in general as an illustration, it would be beneficial for the European Union and its five hundred million citizens, to exclude former managers of these investment banks from any post of financial, budgetary and economic control (ECB, European Commission, National Central Banks). The mixing of these relationships can only lead to even greater confusion between public and private interests, which can only be to the detriment of European public interests. To begin with, the Eurozone should immediately require the Greek government to stop calling on the services of Goldman Sachs.

If the head of Goldman Sachs believes he is « God » as he described himself in a recent interview in 2009, it would be prudent to consider that his bank, and its lookalikes, can seriously behave like devils, and it is therefore wise to draw all the consequences.

To conclude, those who seek where the next sovereign debt crisis will surface: simply look for those states which have called upon Goldman Sachs' services in the last few years and you will have a serious lead!

SOURCE: LEAP E 2020 (2)

(1) A swap is a means by which a borrower can exchange the type of funds he can most easily raise for the type of funds he wants, usually through the intermediary of a bank. For example, a UK company may find it easy to raise a sterling loan when they really want to borrow Deutschmarks; a German company may have exactly the opposite problem. A swap will enable them to exchange the currency they possess for the currency they need. (Oxford Dictionary of Business)

(2) Leap/Europe 2020 (also known as European Laboratory of Political Anticipation) is a think tank established to analyze and anticipate global economic developments from a European perspective and to publish a paid-subscription monthly economic forecast bulletin. It was founded in 1997 among others by Frank Biancheri the founder of the European student network AEGEE(Association des États Generaux de l'Europe) and one of the few pan-European parties,Newropeans. LEAP/E2020 claims to be the first European website of anticipation, independent from any government or lobby.

CHAPTER **8**

Consumerism

'How much is enough? How many houses can you have, how many private jets, how many yachts?'

BUD ASKS GEKKO, THE ICON OF FREE MARKET CAPITALISM, IN *WALL STREET* A MOVIE MADE BY OLIVER STONE

According to the Oxford Dictionary the word 'consumerism' has two different meanings:
1. The protection of consumers' interests.
2. High consumption of goods etc.; belief in this.

An example of the first meaning of this word were the activities of the American Ralph Nader, who was renowned because of his efforts to protect the consumers' interests during the last decades of the 20th century. Among his feats was the fact that he took consumers' matters to court against General Motors.

The second meaning of the word consumerism is important in the context of this chapter. It is the continuous pursuit of more and more goods etc.. And therefore an everlasting need of money to buy whatever is desired. Consumerism is promoted through the constant stimulation of man's material needs. Companies that want to sell their products arouse the desire to do so by means of marketing. Marketing has evolved to a fine-tuned instrument, based on psychology, scanning constantly the entrance to man's mind in order to arouse the urge to buy. It speaks for itself that particularly big companies can afford to invest large sums of money in marketing.

In the U.S. 70% of the GPD was consumed in the year 2007. The consumption per capita in that year was $ 46,000, and that is more than the $ 39,000 income per capita! No wonder that so many Americans suffer under the burden of credit card debts. Also the number of bankruptcies of private households has been huge since the outbreak of the crisis. In 2009 1.4 million private households went bankrupt, and in 2010 until August 900,000. That is 1:125 households in the whole U.S. Joseph Stiglitz, economist and Nobel Prize winner said in an interview in June 2010: In many aspects the present financial-economic situation is worse compared to two years ago. The steps taken by the U.S. Government are by far not sufficient. The deepest point has not been reached yet. Also this year (2010) many Americans will lose their properties. Not to speak of the business real estate sector. There the real problems still have to start. Stiglitz is very much opposed to the idea that a crisis is 'nature's way'. 'This failing system has not developed accidently. The crisis has been created, and was therefore also predictable. In fact, it has been predicted', he said in an interview with *managementbook.nl*.

The situation is not much better, or maybe even worse in the U.K.. In that country the total of personal debts was in £ 1,460 billion in May 2010. The average debt (excluding mortgages) was £ 18,324 per household. The total sum of individual debts is more than what the whole country produces in a year.

Hazardous labour in a factory

The main problem is, that ordinary people get the picture through media such as television, magazines, and movies of what life could be if one had enough money to spend, and that at the same time their income is barely enough to cover the ever increasing expenses. If there is such a thing as a credit card, it is rather tempting to buy some of all these things that promise to make life better. In this context I mention also the peculiar English invention of store credit cards: next to one or more credit cards most people have several store cards on which they can mount up debts at a particular store. Another marketers' trick to create consumer loyalty, whilst causing more private debts.

The ones that are primarily responsible for consumerism are of course we ourselves in our role of consumers. Nevertheless a good deal of the responsibility for all the misery it has caused is also due to companies and banks. Also governments have their part in the total responsibility, by not protecting their citizens against excessive consumption effectively. The complete machinery of production, sales, consumption, and, finally, dumping the product is going on and on. It leads to exhaustion of natural resources, and mountains of waste, often poisonous, because producers generally care more for the qualities a product needs to have (such as shelf life, being fireproof, etc.), than for burdening the environment with the many toxic chemicals added. Also the oil spills, in the Niger Delta, Ecuador, Alaska, and recently in the Gulf of Mexico, push the earth to the brink of an environmental disaster. Of course it is primarily the oil companies that in their rigid strive for shareholder value try to cut expenses as much as possible, even at the cost of safety and preservation of the environment. However, eventually we in our role of consumers have the main responsibility for keeping the circus going.

Child labour in India

Yes, it is serious what we do to our earth. All natural resources are sacrificed on the altar of consumerism. An endless flow of all kinds of goods end after a relatively short period of time on the waste 'mountain'. Of all the things we have bought 95% is cast off within five years. Also the frantic technological development, with, for example, computers, mobile telephones, high definition, blue-ray, wireless applications etc. help the waste mountain grow excessively. This is supported by the producer who stops selling essential parts of the 'old' device after a few years.

In a way we may conclude that consumerism has driven us collectively mad. Personal debts, big financial problems, private bankruptcies, loss of property are the widespread consequences of our collective madness. 'Buy now, pay later', 'Do not worry, you can use the credit card' 'Take a second mortgage on your house' and so on are methods used to stimulate us to buy, the new well equipped kitchen, the latest LCD screen, the I Pad, and many more things presented to us by the welfare economy.

Apart from this, there is what we might call the hidden economy. Massive amounts of money are spent in this area of sex, drugs and gambling. This type of consumerism has brought forward its own 'money cycle' of grey and black money. There is also the worldwide fast-growing gaming industry. It is said that in 2009 $ 100 billion were spent all over the world.

I am not claiming here that we should abandon all technological achievements. Many of them have helped us to live a more comfortable life. Although there are also technological developments that may be qualified as 'over the edge' strictly spoken unnecessary, or even bad for our health and that of animals. Wise consumption is primarily a matter of consciousness. We should realize ourselves that we are the ones that decide to buy or not. We do not have to let ourselves be pushed into buying by whatever marketing message, for example that our life is not complete if we do not have this or that.

As socially responsible consumers, we should be aware what the product has been made of, where it comes from, if child labour or absurdly low wages involved in the production etc. It is in our hands to stop the craziness of companies that look for production of their goods at ever lower expense, and therefore at the cost of people, resources, and environment. It is up to us to turn to sustainable consumption which does not harm the production resources.

Dark clouds over the credit card business

10 MARCH 2009, SOURCE: *HET FINANCIEEL DAGBLAD*

More headaches await U.S. banks with big credit card divisions. Increasing unemployment implicates growing uncollectible credit card debts. In February 2009 CEO Ken Lewis of the Bank of America informed Congress that 2009 is going to be a devastating year for the credit card business (true, there were more than 1.4 million bankruptcies in 2009).

Banks have money available to absorb losses, however it is a question mark if this will do. In December 2008 the potential loss was estimated at 7.7%. This percentage might increase as more and more Americans become unemployed. The number of unemployed people is the best marker for future credit card losses. It is a common rule that the % of unemployed is increased by 1% (in 2010 the unemployment % increased above 10%). Especially large bank corporations should be worried. According to credit rating institute Moody's $ 46 billion of the total $ 76 billion is attributable to Bank of America, JP Morgan Chase, and Citigroup.

OTHER OPTIONS

Insulating old houses means that our natural resources supplies in gas and oil will be sustained. Solar panels and heat pumps in as many as possible houses would further sustain our energy supplies. It is in the interest of our whole society to pay full attention to the development of durable energy (for example solar, wind, tide, waterpower). If we would collectively decide to invest on a large scale in the development of durable energy, and simply set aside the doom prophecy of companies such as Shell (There Is No Alternative for fossil energy) we would create a very important basis for a better future for the earth and for our children.

We have become so used to a world wherein oil, gas, and all products made on the basis of oil play a very important role, that we simply cannot imagine a world where fossil energy plays a by-role. Furthermore, there are many stakeholders in the oil and gas revenues. Governments of oil-producing countries, oil producing companies, oil-selling companies (often but not always the same as oil-producing companies), governments of countries that consume oil, companies that transport oil etc. From the revenue in the U.S., 4% is for the transporters, 4% for the gas stations, 8% for the refinery, 12% for the government, and 72% for the oil companies (upstream and downstream). It depends whether companies such as Exxon and Shell have their own oilfields, and in which country they have those fields which part of the revenue is theirs to keep. For example, in Russia, the government demands half of the revenue. This is why oil companies are inclined to look for territories that are not owned by interfering governments.

In Europe governments are real big money makers. Not by demanding part of the revenue of oil companies, but by taxing citizens (excise duties, V.A.T.) For example, in France the government receives 50% of the price one pays at the pump, in Germany even 60%. No wonder that governments are not very much inclined to give up such a profitable arrangement. No wonder that shortsighted politicians do not want to invest at large scale in environmentally friendly and durable energy. As we are the consumers of the energy products, collectively we are in the position to demand more investments in the development of durable energy from our governments. Here again we should realize our position as the ones it is all about.

If China, India, and Brazil keep on developing the way they do, the demand for energy will rise by 45% in 2030. The consequences of this are far beyond our imagination. It is not a world we have in mind for our children. This illustrates how bad we need a sustainable economy based on durable energy.

One of the many initiatives to develop such an economy came out of a British student project. It is called Transition Towns:

> The main aim of the project generally, and echoed by the Towns locally, is to raise awareness of sustainable living and build local ecological resilience in the near future. Communities are encouraged to seek out methods for reducing energy usage as well as reducing their reliance on long supply chains that are totally dependent on fossil fuels for essential items. Food is a key area, and they often talk of "Food feet, not food miles!" Initiatives so far have included creating community gardens to grow food; business waste exchange, which seeks to match the waste of one industry with another industry that uses this waste; and even simply repairing old items rather than throwing them away. The Transition Network website contains an initial listing of projects that initiatives have started up.

> While the focus and aims remain the same, the methods used to achieve these vary. For example, Totnes has introduced its own local currency, the Totnes Pound, which is redeemable in local shops and businesses, helping to reduce "food miles" while also supporting local firms. This idea is also planned to be introduced in three Welsh

transition towns and in Maleny, Australia, the Baroon Dollar as a part of a regional transition towns project.

Central to the Transition Town movement is the idea that a life without oil could in fact be far more enjoyable and fulfilling than the present: "by shifting our mind-set we can actually recognise the coming post-cheap oil era as an opportunity rather than a threat, and design the future low carbon age to be thriving, resilient and abundant — somewhere much better to live than our current alienated consumer culture based on greed, war and the myth of perpetual growth." An essential aspect of Transition in many places, is that the outer work of transition needs to be matched by inner transition. That is in order to move down the energy descent pathways effectively we need to rebuild our relations with our selves, with each other and with the "natural" worlds. That requires focusing on the heart and soul of transition.

SOURCE: THE TRANSITION HANDBOOK, 2008, ROB HOPKINS

Hopefully more and more people will recognize initiatives like Transition Towns as a very rational and down-to-earth way to create more hope for the future.

As I said before, we have been stuffed with products that we had to have to make our life complete. In spite of within five years this, 95% of those badly wanted products end up on the ever-growing waste mountain, for a big part stashed away in 'developing' countries, where they often cause serious health problems. Nevertheless, there are initiatives that offer a better solution, and that should be considered very seriously. One of them is the 'cradle to cradle' philosophy:

In their book *Cradle to Cradle*, McDonough and Braungart argue that the conflict between industry and the environment is not an indictment of commerce but an outgrowth of purely opportunistic design. The design of products and manufacturing systems growing out of the Industrial Revolution reflected the spirit of the day-and yielded a host of unintended yet tragic consequences. Today, with our growing knowledge of the living earth, design can reflect a new spirit. In fact, the authors write, when designers employ the intelligence of natural systems—the effectiveness of nutrient cycling, the abundance of the sun's energy—they can create products, industrial systems, buildings, even regional plans that allow nature and commerce to fruitfully co-exist.

Cradle to Cradle maps the lineaments of McDonough and Braungart's new design paradigm, offering practical steps on how to innovate within today's economic environment. Part social history, part green business primer, part design manual, the book makes plain that the re-invention of human industry is not only within our grasp, it is our best hope for a future of sustaining prosperity. In addition to describing the hopeful, nature-inspired design principles that are making industry both prosperous and sustainable, the book itself is a physical symbol of the changes to come. It is printed on a synthetic 'paper,' made from plastic resins and inorganic fillers, designed to look and feel like top quality paper while also being waterproof and rugged. And the book can be easily recycled in localities with systems to collect polypropylene, like that in yogurt containers. This 'treeless' book points the way toward the day when synthetic books, like many other products, can be used, recycled, and used again without losing any material quality—in cradle to cradle cycles.

SOURCE: WWW.WISEGEEK.COM

Undoubtedly there will be many hurdles on the road to success for initiatives like this one. However, it is most important that effort is given to creating a sustainable economy.

Last but not least, consumers could make a major contribution to the establishment of sustainable consumption by supporting and reinforcing small and medium sized businesses all over the world. Buying products from SMEs, especially those which are innovative and produce durable goods, means giving a boost to regional economies and to the creation of quality employment. In fact there should be easily accessible international internet websites that inform consumers about the products and services SMEs offer. One of the weak points of SMEs is that they generally do not have enough capital available for promotion. Internet offers an opportunity that could turn this weakness into a strength.

More about credit cards:

Despite warnings of a potential double dip recession, banks are presenting struggling customers with offers of cheaper debt than they made available before the 2007 economic crash. Experts warned that Britain could face a new "credit card boom" leaving families heavily in debt as they borrow to make ends meet and struggle to pay off the money. It comes amid concerns of future job losses, particulary as the Coalition government's spending cuts are due to take effect.

The research, from two price comparison websites, found some banks were offering credit cards with attractive interest free rates for an introductory period of an average of 12.2 months. This was longer than during the peak of the last credit boom but once they end leave families with high interest repayments. While the improved rates are good in the short term, it can be costly for those who still have debts when introductory offers run out. Other offers from banks, which have announced recent profits of more than £16 billion, offered cash rebates and other incentives to spend on credit such as attractive interest-free "balance transfer" deals, which encourage borrowers to move debt between cards.

There was also some evidence that despite tightening the rules on who they would lend money to during the recession, the criteria was now being relaxed. It came as figures from the Office for Budget Responsibility estimated that the average British family of four will borrow £24,000 more during over next five years. It predicted household debt will top £1.8 billion by 2015.

Martin Lewis, an analyst at consumer website moneysavingexpert. com, warned consumers to handle the current deals with care. "Debt is like fire, used well it is a great tool, used badly you'll get burned," he said. "The worst thing to do with a credit card is to use it to fill the gaps your income does not meet each month, that will see borrowings constantly grow and can leave you in a debt spiral." Kevin Mountford, head of banking at moneysupermarket. com, added: "While interest-free periods may be getting longer, the sting in the tail is that the rates of interest charged once they end are also increasing." Ministers have said they will review lending and borrowing schemes.

SOURCE: TELEGRAPH.CO.UK 23 AUGUST 2010

CHAPTER 9

Complementary currency

Whenever a crisis occurs, small and medium-sized companies come under pressure. They are the first ones to lose sales. Because of their size it is not easy to diversify. That means that it is not easy to sell products that are more successful under these circumstances. SMEs also have a limited amount of capital available to invest in new opportunities. Because of their already smaller size, SMEs have great difficulties in downsizing the business. For example, they cannot close an unsuccessful division or stop activities in a country that does not offer enough profit, like multinational corporations can. Yet SMEs are the backbone of the economy of most developed and developing countries, and also the main suppliers of employment.

SMEs and entrepreneurs play a significant role in all economies and are the key generators of employment and income, and drivers of innovation and growth. In the OECD area, SMEs employ more than half of the labour force in the private sector. In the European Union, they account for over 99 % of all enterprises. Furthermore, 91 % of

> these enterprises are micro-firms with less than 10 workers. Given
> their importance in all economies, they are essential for the eco-
> nomic recovery.
>
> OECD REPORT 2009

According to the OECD, these small and medium-sized companies are essential for the economic recovery. Nevertheless, their financial position is placed under great pressure, because for their financial funding SMEs rely to great extent on short-term bank credit and supplier's credit. And both types of credit are extremely difficult to get. Government support is often based on guarantees or subsidies for long-term investment, especially for SMEs that offer a convincing business plan with a realistic prospect of future profits. This is not for struggling SMEs with dropping sales, and due to that, losses. Unfortunately, these SMEs are much bigger in numbers than those with good prospects. Generally their position is not due to mismanagement, as bankers let us try to believe, but to failing demand. Unemployment, lower wages, high private debts, expense cuttings in (semi-)government organizations are some of the reasons for that.

For many SMEs it is merely a matter of surviving and hoping that the crisis will be over soon. However, there are exceptions. The most exciting one was in Switzerland in 1934. Under similar circumstances as in this present time, SME entrepreneurs in that country were also confronted with inaccessibility of bank and suppliers credit. Sixteen of those entrepreneurs came together and decided that it was unacceptable that the economic process was totally obstructed through scarcity of money, at least scarce for them. They decided to establish a bank that brought its own currency in circulation: the WIR (which means 'we'). The WIR was supposed to make transactions between businesses possible, when the scarcity of Swiss Francs obstructed them. Thus, the WIR was a business-to-business currency, and existed alongside the Swiss Franc. Therefore the WIR was a complementary currency.

An example of how the WIR was applied was the building of a hotel. Only 60% of the building costs could be financed in Swiss Francs, for more the bank was not willing to take the risk. The remaining 40% was financed with WIR. The WIR was paid to a company that accepted WIR, and also was a member of the Cooperative WIR Bank organisation. For example, the supplier of building materials was a member of the Cooperation. This company was willing to accept 40% of the payment in WIR, and 60% in Swiss Francs. Consequently the building materials supplier could spend its WIR on the purchase of new delivery vans from a car dealer who was also a member of the Cooperation.

The system worked miraculously. It helped the Swiss SMEs through the big crisis, and also through the more recent ones. Certainly part of the legendary stability of the Swiss Economy is due to the WIR. Today there are 60,000 members, which is a lot of the total number of 300,000 SMEs in Switzerland. September 2010 the RAI Italy broadcasted a television documentary about the WIR. A spokesman of the WIR Bank said in that program that also in these troubled times the system proves its usefulness. Sales of the 60,000 member SMEs are by average 10% higher than their colleague non-member SMEs.

Of course there are also drawbacks in the WIR system. This open letter from Susan Witt from the E.F. Schumacher Society U.S.A., written in 2008 is clear about them:

> Just got back from another Rotary meeting in Basel. You know me, I don't hesitate to explore what is on my mind, so of course asked everyone at my table and others about WIR. One of my table mates is a contractor. He said that if you are in the trades, there is no question that you must take WIR. At a minimum 15% per job. The WIR bank is making mortgages in WIR at 1%. That of course encourages building and renovation, providing jobs for contractors. But as a contractor, he is not thinking of the bigger economic question, just

the inconvenience of having to take WIR because he is limited in where he can spend it. One hotel in the area takes 100% WIR and he says they have a lot of business, especially from contractors who are looking for outlets for their WIR.

But he is one of those without a WIR account. So he black markets them. Meaning he takes a WIR check, but an undesignated check and passes it on like cash. Of course when a business knows that it is black marketed, they won't take it at full value. They have an advantage in the negotiation. The business that wants to deposit it, then signs it. I'm assuming that is especially businesses with mortgages in WIR, who need WIR to pay back the mortgage. The trouble for the person without a WIR account is the end of the year – you cannot carry them over on your books if they are unsigned and you don't have an account to put them in. So especially at the end of the year there is a huge black market trade in WIR (according to this contractor). He said those who want WIR for building or a specific purpose can find WIR at a 40% discount at year's end.

Can't understand why these guys don't just open a WIR account – it would be easier than all there under the table deals. Another person at my table was an accountant. Now of course he only deals with legitimate trade in WIR. He wants to see WIR in an account. But he says, even so, his firm when they see WIR on the books discount it by 20%. So if there is 10,000 WIR in the account, they value it at 8000 francs. If the business owner turns it to better account, that is all to the good, but they don't take it for granted. The limitation on where it can be spent, devalues it in their eyes. Another guy builds waste water treatment centers for towns and cities. Because he works with government entities, he does not trade in WIR. But his opinion is that in this troubled economic time, WIR is proving the better currency.

Just gathering data while here. Certainly the hotel likes it, but then they had the advantage of the low cost mortgage and they see an advantage in taking 50% WIR for the rooms. There is always repair work to be done, and the contractors are used to having WIR payments specified in the contract. The hotel has more limited places to spend WIR relative to food sources, so only takes 15% WIR in the restaurant.

The contractor likes the idea that BerkShares is convertible back to federal dollars, even if at a discount. That would give more flexibility in his eyes. If WIR had some convertibility, other than black market, he would like it better

SOURCE: E.F. SCHUMACHER INSTITUTE U.S.A. 2008

Three things are vital for the future success of complementary money.

Firstly, *complementary money should be convertible back into the official currency.* You can borrow or buy WIR to make a transaction possible that would not have taken place if a complementary currency had not been in place. But once a company has accepted WIR as a medium of payment, they have to spend it elsewhere, because WIR cannot be converted back into Swiss Francs. Apparently except for on the black market, apparently, where it can be exchanged into Swiss Francs at a big discount. Yet, many businesses prefer to make use of this black market instead of spending WIR within the cooperation. The idea to increase spending within the circle of members of the WIR Bank does not work for them because these entrepreneurs do not want to be pressed into buying products or services they would not have bought if they had a free choice.

Secondly, *the basis for products and services that SMEs offer in a complementary currency cooperation is broad and diverse.* Buyers in a complementary currency cooperation should have a choice out of more suppliers of the same product or service. In other words, there should be a healthy competition. And this is of course a problem, especially in the first years of a new cooperation when the idea still has to be settled.

Thirdly, *taxes and wages should be paid in a complementary currency.* The Swiss government, for example, does not accept tax payments and wages be paid by businesses in WIR. Yet, more and more Swiss consumers use WIR, for a part, as currency for their purchases of products and services.

The conclusion is that complementary currency works, and also supports the economy, especially SMEs, in times of crisis, which has been proven by the success of the WIR. However, this money has some serious drawbacks that could only be overcome if national governments and/or the European Union would actively support the setting up of a complementary currency system. Furthermore, on a large scale SMEs have to be aware of the need for a complementary currency. If the system is sabotaged like it is in Switzerland by the entrepreneurs themselves, it will not develop to its full potential. Perhaps as long as the Swiss Franc, and any other currency, is not really scarce yet, entrepreneurs keep having their doubts. However, the problem is that if the crisis deepens and money indeed becomes scarce, it may be too late to launch a WIR-like solution.

The WIR may be classified as a barter based exchange model, introduced on a national scale. Barter, because central in the system is the exchange of goods and services between members of the WIR Bank Cooperation.

Other solutions to minimize the role of traditional money can be found in Electronic Trading Tools. The Internet and other new technologies such as "smart cards" have opened the possibility of trading without use of traditional forms of money. Many inventive individuals are suggesting ways of linking these electronic cards, which are primarily tools to facilitate consumer credit, to businesses with defined missions, such as merchants of green products. The majority of these applications are still on the drawing board, but their developers have imagined including aspects of customer loyalty notes and other discount benefits as incentives for consumers to join. Most are denominated in US dollars, though The Terra Trade Reference Currency proposed by Bernard Lietaer is exploring an electronic trading card with transactions denominated in a basket of commodities held by global corporations.

Bernard Lietaer can be considered as the 'founding father' of complementary currencies. In 2001 he published *The Future of Money*. In the introduction he shows his vision on money and why there should be a change. This is a fragment from the introduction:

- Your money's value is determined by a **global casino** of unprecedented proportions: $2 trillion are traded per day in foreign exchange markets, 100 times more than the trading volume of all the stockmarkets of the world combined. *Only 2% of these foreign exchange transactions relate to the "real" economy reflecting movements of real goods and services in the world, and 98% are purely speculative.* This global casino is triggering the foreign exchange crises which shook Mexico in 1994-5, Asia in 1997 and Russia in 1998. These emergencies are the dislocation symptoms of the old Industrial Age money system. *Unless some precautions are taken soon, there is at least a 50-50 chance that the next five to ten years will see a global money meltdown, the only plausible way for a global depression.*
- The Information Age has already spawned new kinds of currencies: frequent flyer miles are evolving toward a "corporate scrip" (a private currency issued by a corporation) for the traveling elite; a giant corporation you never heard of is issuing its own "Netmarket Cash" for Internet commerce; even Alan Greenspan, Chairman of the Federal Reserve, foresees "new private currency markets in the 21st century."

- Exorbitant compensations are paid to the very few at the top: it started with movie stars and sports heroes, and has now spread to top lawyers, traders, doctors, and business leaders. In the 1960's CEO's salaries were only thirty times greater than those of the average worker, compared with two hundred times today. *Is this the dawn of a society where "Winner-takes-all" or a short-term last gasp of the transition out of the Industrial Age?*
- 1,900 local communities in the world (2.100 in 2010), including over a hundred in the US, were in 2001 issuing their own currency , independently from the national money system. Some communities, like in Ithaca, New York, issue paper currency; others in Canada, Australia, the UK or France issue complementary electronic money.

This visionary book, written in 2001 predicted a global money meltdown 'unless precautions were taken'. Now in 2010 the first meltdown took place at the end of 2007. And because basically nothing has changed since, the second even more devastating meltdown is likely to come. The problems with the euro, yen, sterling, and dollar are multiple. Now, the focus is on the euro because of the problems in Greece and other participating countries in the euro zone. Our attention is temporarily distracted from the other 'big currencies'. However, they all suffer from the same deadly disease that might be characterized as complete exhaustion. The final collapse of the money system is presumably unpleasantly near, despite all efforts of governments to postpone it.

The local communities referred to by Bernard Lietaer, perhaps offer a better chance than the large scale bartering and electronic solutions. The big advantage is that the initiatives come forth from communities themselves. Therefore they have a solid basis. Maybe the diversity of these local currency systems is also an advantage. Similar to nature bio diversity enforces a biotope; financial diversity helps to make an economy stronger. Where systems may fail because of structural drawbacks, local currencies might be successful on the long term, because they can develop organically, on the basis of trial-and-error. However, cooperation and interconnectivity are the magic words. Too little cooperation and lack of interconnectivity will lead to chaos. Everywhere in the world, e.g. U.S., the U.K., Germany, The Netherlands, Italy, and Brazil, local currency initiatives can be found.

Two examples illustrate how local currencies work:

The BerkShare in the U.S.:

> The purpose of BerkShares is to function on a local scale the same way that national currencies have functioned on a national scale—building the local economy by maximizing circulation of trade within a defined region. Widely used in the early 1900s, local currencies are again being recognized as a tool for sustainable economic development. The currency distinguishes the local businesses that accept the currency from those that do not, building stronger relationships and a greater affinity between the business community and the citizens of a particular place.

> The people who choose to use the currency make a conscious commitment to buy local first. They are taking personal responsibility for the health and well-being of their community by laying the foundation of a truly vibrant, thriving local economy. BerkShares will not, and are not intended to, replace federal currency. Their use will help strengthen the regional economy, favoring locally owned enterprises, local manufacturing, and local jobs, and reducing the region's dependence on an unpredictable global economy.

> **How are BerkShares placed in circulation?**
> BerkShares are placed in circulation when citizens exchange federal dollars for BerkShares at any of the BerkShares Exchange Banks (see list below). Some restrictions may apply. Citizens may exchange

federal dollars for BerkShares at any of the BerkShare Exchange Banks during normal bank hours (some restrictions may apply): The exchange rate is ninety-five cents per BerkShare. Ninety-five federal dollars will yield one hundred BerkShares. BerkShares are printed in 1, 5, 10, 20, and 50 denominations of BerkShares. Federal dollars remain on deposit at the BerkShare Exchange Banks to redeem excess BerkShares at a five percent discount. 100 BerkShares would be exchanged for ninety -five federal dollars.

SOURCE: WWW.BERKSHARES.ORG

The Chiemgauer in Germany:

In 583 businesses, clients can choose whether they would like to pay with Euro or with Chiemgauers. The Chiemgauer is a local currency that has been conceived, designed, promoted and brought into circulation by six girls, students of the local Waldorf high school in Prien and their teacher, Christian Gelleri. Currently, there are 489,595 chiemgauer in circulation. Bundles of 50 chiemgauer, sorted by denomination and held together by a rubber band, are available 43 servicepoints. Those who want to use it pay 50 euro for a bundle and spend them in the shops that accept the chiemgauer.

SOURCE: WWW.CHIEMGAUER.INFO

These examples are just two out of many more. There is a wide diversity, everywhere with the same purpose, to sustain the local economy. Nevertheless, there is a big danger hidden in local currencies. The exchange of goods and services over the regio's borders might be obstructed by them. Sustaining the local economy is a good thing, over-protecting it may result in an adversary effect. Therefore, if the 'big money system' collapses, it will be a good thing that people can depend on strong local or regional economies. However, this should never lead to isolationism. Internet offers the chances to interconnect the local or regional communities, and may be a big help to sustain the national and international economy, based on the strength of them. This could be the start of a totally different globalization. Not one based on the exploitation and exhaustion of resources all over the world, but on the welfare and strength of local economies.

This example may illustrate how it could work:
China has produced an enormous growth in their economy. In 1980 China's GDP was just 2% of the total World's GDP. In 2006 it had increased to 10.1%, and the estimate is a further growth to 14.7% in 2013. This powerful growth has been particularly due to export. The price China has to pay for this growth is a big damage to the environment. Focused on low-cost production as China has been, investments in improving the environment lagged behind. Yet there is an increasing need, especially in the big cities, for a better quality of life. Cleaner air, water and reducing the use of polluting materials are the main requirements. There is a growing awareness in China that further growth will be obstructed if the environment keeps on degrading. Therefore, initiatives to improve environment from the Chinese government as well as from private companies have been taken.

A Chinese trading company, for example, has done extensive research on SMEs in Europe that develop and produce environment-protecting products. They have chosen for SMEs because their potential clients in China are also SMEs. These are SMEs such as car repair garages, clothing shops, furniture workshops, and machine construction companies. The philosophy of this Chinese trading organization is that SMEs have a better understanding of the specific problems of other SMEs, and that the ecological products they develop are more tuned to the needs of their clients. This Chinese trading company, Xu Trading Shanghai, has composed a shortlist of three companies out of over two thousand European SMEs, one in Sweden, one in Germany, and one in The Netherlands. This is a fine example of 'think global, act local', and a great opportunity for innovative SMEs.

CHAPTER 10

Money and Value

The main driving force behind the financial system is the continuous trade-off between risk and return. Investors always seek to balance the amount of risk they are willing to accept and the expected return on investment. The bigger the risk, the higher the expected return. There is always a limit to the risk an investor is willing to take. Banks, for example, should be risk avoiding, because of their financial structure. Their debt is much higher than their equity, technically expressed as a high leverage. Losses on loans to customers have a direct impact on the financial position of banks. The relatively small equity of the bank will be gone soon if they have to write-off huge amounts of the loans granted.

Because of the limited risk, banks require a relatively low return on loans compared to that what an investor in shares requires of a business with high risk perceived. Therefore as long as they do what they are supposed to do, banks will never ask relatively high returns on their investments in loans. Yet, during the past decades banks have

moved from their conservative positions in the direction of a more
investor- like approach. Attracted by the high returns big commercial
banks have been acting more and more as investment bankers. However, there has been just one big difference with the private investor.
Banks conduct their business with money that is not theirs, whilst private investors take risks with money that is basically their own.

What banks actually did was go for short term profit, at the same time
covering up the increasing risks. The constructs they invented to cam-
ouflage the bad news were smart if not cunning. The good news was
prominently displayed. For example pension funds all over the world
purchased huge amounts of collateralized debt obligations (CDOs),
because of their high return combined with low risk. That is, seemingly because institutes such as Moody's mentioned above gave them
mainly a triple A (= excellent) status. As long as things went well in

the booming economy of the past decades, profits were huge for the bankers and their shareholders. All financial products, whether they were collateralized debt obligations, credit default swaps or any other creation designed by the financial 'wizards' brought lots of money in the short term, and at the same time lots of risk in the long term.

The financial crisis in 2007 seemingly made an end to the long years of misuse. Taxpayers' money saved the banks in many countries all over the world. That is, for the time being. Since basically nothing has changed after the financial crisis, and banks went on to do business as usual the second outburst may be expected, even in the short term.

In August 2010 the Canadian economist William White, chairman of the Economic and Development Review Committee, OECD, said in an interview with the Dutch paper *Het Financieele Dagblad*:

> To be honest I would be amazed if there would not be a second crisis. The factors that have lead to the first crisis are still present. Too high private debts, (extremely) high leverages in the financial sector, instabilities in world trade to name a few. Nobody can claim there is a solid economic recovery in the western countries. We have had a short-lived upturn, mainly due to financial government support. Furthermore, companies pushed up their inventory to normal levels. However, nowhere companies invested firmly. Multinationals, especially U.S. corporations have lots of cash available, and make big profits at the moment. Nevertheless they are very reluctant to make investment decisions.'

William White is concerned about a second crisis. Though in his view a deep crisis might be necessary to make a new and better start, he indicates that they have caused huge political and social problems, and even wars in the past. The instabilities William White talks about are due to the behaviour of banks, but also to that of private investors. The latter also seek high returns combined with as low as possible risks. The richer a private investor, the more tools he has to reach that goal. The hedge funds mentioned before accept only investors with very high incomes and capitals. The reason for that is obvious. The more an investor has, the better the hedge fund can rule out risks. For that purpose they have a multitude of tools available, for example, swaps, caps, collars etc.. In this context I will not discuss this further. You might say that hedge funds are generally always on the winning side, regardless the state of the economy.

Stock exchanges have become more of a casino than a meeting place between investors and companies that seek capital. Investors are mainly not interested in the company they put their money into. The profit between buying and selling is the interest of most investors. The nervous trade over the past decades in shares, options and other financial products aimed at short term success, has also caused much instability.

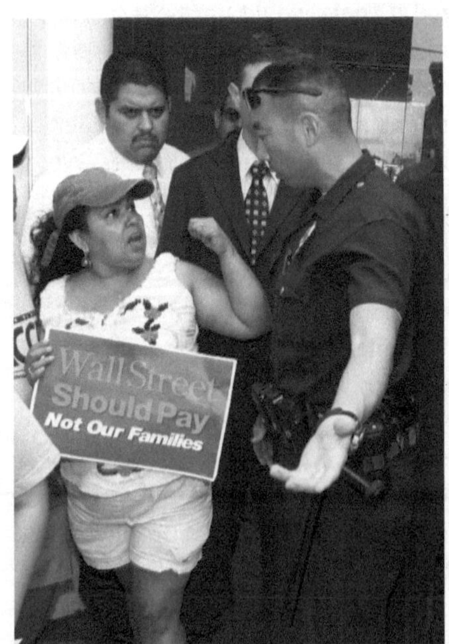

A protester is blocked by police and bank officials as she tries to enter to demand that Wall Street banks repay what protesters claim the bailout debt that they owe the people.
A recent report said the US Treasury Department expects to recover all but 42 billion dollars of the 370 billion it has lent to troubled US banks since the financial crisis began in 2008.

The results of the large pharmaceutical corporation Novartis under-lines the distance between the investor in shares and the reality of the company itself. In 2009 Novartis made a profit of $ 8.4 billion. At the end of 2009 there were 2,267,855,586 (more than 2.2 billion) shares in circulation. All those shares are at bearer, which means that you cannot identify who owns them. Novartis paid out more than 52% of their profit to the shareholders in dividends or *$ 4.5 billion*. A huge amount of money. However, this is just $ 1.95 per share. The price per share for Novartis shares is around $ 53.50. The return on invest-ment for an investor that bought the share for that price is 3.6%. This shows how the dilution of mega profits into small returns works.

It speaks for itself that investors of 'the first hour' who bought their shares many years ago for a relatively low price, earn a lot on their investment. Often these investors hold a relatively large number of shares in one or more corporations. The mega number of total shares issued by nearly all big corporations is to their advantage, because they can stay hidden as long as the shares they hold do not exceed a substantial interest, generally 5%, for Novartis more than 113.4 million shares. Furthermore, there are constructs to spread the shares over more trusts, funds, foundations, etc.. These shareholders also ex-ert influence on the companies' management via these vehicles. This is how the financial elite has established its position in the real economy.

On Thursday **Warren Buffet** paid up on his annual charity luncheon event. Attending was Zhao Danyang, a Chinese Hedge Fund man-ager who donated $2.11 million to one of Mr. Buffet's favorite chari-ties in return for the privilege of inviting 7 friends and relatives to lunch with the Oracle of Omaha at Smith and Wollensky in NYC. Zhao, an astute and long term investor in China through his $130 million hedge fund, has generated 600% returns over the past 6 years. Zhao views Buffet as his teacher, and has credited him with the inspiration required to be a successful investor. Perhaps there's a lesson here for all of us- the longer term view might be the way to generate real wealth, if we can take a cue for Mr. Buffet and Mr. Zhao. During the lunch, The Oracle commented Mr. Zhao is lucky to be living in the "Era of Chinese Ascendancy". Buffet stated he believes the next few decades in China will provide the same kinds of opportunities the last few decades provided Mr. Buffet in the United States.

SOURCE: OTC JOURNAL 29 JUNE 2009

For smaller investors the stock exchange is no more than a big casino, with a bigger chance of losses than profits. The price of shares is so high compared to the real value of them that the only chance to get positive results is to gamble on positive margins between selling and buying. This pertains to shares as well as to options. The last few years have proven again that this game sorts out more disappointment than luck. Greed, short-sightedness, selfishness have made a monster of the financial system. The aftermath of the present crisis has proven that basically nothing has changed. Therefore I share William White's view that if a complete change in awareness does not develop, the whole economy might be destroyed completely.

I have used several times the term 'the real economy'. What is it in fact? The real economy might be defined as the process of all goods and services produced by organisations/businesses, and consequently, bought by consumers. The goods and services produced should have value for the buyer, otherwise he or she would not be inclined to buy. For example, if a theatre company produces a play, there has to be interest in the play, or the company is not successful. If the number of visitors is as expected, the theatre company has apparently created value. Another example is a new business that introduces a environmentally friendly produced bio-fuel. If there are enough buyers willing to pay the relatively high price for this fuel, the new business has created value.

The second question is: who is 'the business' or 'the theatre company' or 'the hospital' etc.? Any organisation can only exist because of the people that work for it. Even in organisations that are automated to a high extent, people are at the basis of the value creation that takes place in it. Consequently, organisations can be regarded as by people driven *value chains*.

> A value chain can be defined as the chain of activities by which a company buys in materials, creates a good or service, markets it, and provides services after a sale is made. Each step creates more value for the consumer.
>
> There are five value-creating activities:
> - Inbound distribution
> - Operations
> - Outbound distribution
> - Marketing
> - After-sales service
>
> And four supporting activities:
> - Buying
> - Research & development
> - Human resource management
> - Facilities management
>
> **SOURCE:** OXFORD DICTIONARY OF BUSINESS

If you examine the activities, they are all driven by people within the organisation, regardless of the level of automation of the processes, and not by money. Not by loans from banks, neither from money from investors in equity. *Money does not create value.* Why then do investors require such a big part of all the value added by an organisation? Oil and gas company Shell, for instance, earned $19.1 billion for its shareholders and paid $ 10.6 billion to its staff (including top management) in 2009; food company Unilever paid € 5.2 billion to its employees and earned in the bad year 2009 its shareholders € 4.1

billion. In the year 2007 when the financial crisis hit the world bank corporation HSBC earned $20.5 billion for its shareholders and paid $ 18.5 billion to its staff.

Apparently we do think that investors are more entitled to the value added of a company than the employees are. Because we collectively believe that money can make money, it happens the way it does. There are just a few who wonder why people do not receive a bigger part of the value created by them instead of the money providers. Also peculiar is the distribution of incomes within a company. This is completely uneven. The board of management in most of the corporations earn 50-60 times more money than the other employees. This underlines that not only shareholders, but also those who guard the shareholders value get the bigger part of the value added.

Not all shareholder/owners of companies have the same idea about what they are entitled to because of their ownership. An example of someone who had a different view on this was Scott Bader in the U.K. In 1951 the Swiss Ernest Bader gave all his shares in the company (his wife's name is Scott, hence the company's name Scott Bader), owned by him and his wife, to the collectivity of their employees. The trust in which all the shares were put were called a commonwealth, making clear that the gains in shareholder value were for the benefit of all employees. Bader was convinced that capital should not be the owner of labour. In his vision earning money with money leads to inequality, jealousy and conflicts. Furthermore, he decided that the ratio of the highest wages to the lowest should not be more than 7:1, which is in sharp contrast to today's practice in many organizations.

Bader also tried to educate the employees in what today is called social governance. They were entitled to 40% of the net profit. However half of this amount was destined to contribute to projects in developing countries, for example a clean water project in Africa. The employees could choose which project they wanted to contribute to. The other half of the 40% was to be paid out to the employees at year's end.

The remaining 60% of the profit was retained in the business to make the company financially stronger and more independent of banks. According to the website www.scotbader.com the original socio-economic ideas of Ernest Bader have survived the nearly sixty years since the creation of the commonwealth, and the company is still lively in business. Today Scott Bader employs 600 people worldwide, and has manufacturing sites in Europe, Middle East, and South Africa. The turnover is € 220 million (2010).

It is surprising that so little attention has been paid to this successful experiment. It has proven that the separation between capital and labour is not 'nature's way'. It only serves those who want capital 'to work for them'. But have you ever seen a euro, a pound, or a dollar working? The idea that people who create value are entitled to the returns it gives, was brought into practice by Ernest Bader. By doing this he was far ahead of his time.

Today reluctantly some companies allow their employees to participate in the companies' capital. And those who have decided this are generally not disappointed about the decision. The number of Dutch companies that offer employee participation in their capital has been doubled during the last ten years, concludes Eric Kaarsemaker in research done for the University of York (U.K.) Those companies experienced an improved motivation and commitment by their employees.

Another example of the value chain approach wherein the employees and not shareholders nor management play the leading part is Semco. The Brazilian Ricardo Semler was more than twenty years ago at the age of 22 years appointed as CEO in the family business Semco. Semco was an old-fashioned machine manufacturer when Ricardo Semler took over. During the first years of his management Ricardo continued the business approach of his father. He was just 25 when Ricardo Semler was hit by a severe burn-out. It lasted a year before he recovered. Back in business he had three intentions:

- No mix of business and private life.
- Just do what you really believe in.
- Don't wait until you are old to enjoy your retirement. The idea is that you can take advantage of it once a week, from any age.

The basis of his altered attitude was the awareness that his employees were the backbone of the business. By really treating them as grown-up people, who can take their own responsibilities, make their own decisions, are creative if they are not drowned in codes of conduct and accountability, the organisation he had in his mind could develop. During the years that followed, everything was under discussion, nothing had to stay as it was. Step by step Ricardo Semler democratised Semco, resulting in a completely flat, non-hierarchical organisation.

In an interview about this process that took many years, Ricardo Semler said: 'If people act like caged animals it is not the people but the cage that causes that behaviour. It is not in the human nature to wonder who to ask permission for anything continuously. It is all about trusting people. However this is a difficult and long process because of the long time of working in an environment where everything is based on mistrust and control.'

The question how to democratise an organization was answered by Ricardo Semler as follows: ' A democratic organization is not a matter of a one-day decision. We are already a quarter of a century in a day-to-day learning process. It is a very time consuming process, whilst the conditioning of people is very profound.' People have to learn how to develop as free and creative beings. The most important thing is that those who are leading such a process repeatedly tell them that 'nothing is because it is'. Anything is open for discussion. For example, why have a head office accepting a loss of time and health through long traffic jams, when people can work at home and communicate through internet? Or, why should people be managed by someone higher in the hierarchy if they are perfectly able to cooperate and make decisions without a leader? Semco has taken leave of the old-fashioned controller-style manager. Managers have a coordinating role, and their performance is evaluated by the employees. Furthermore, Semco is organized in small autonomous units. The basic idea is that a manager is not able to manage hundreds of people in a humane way. That is, not by numbers, targets, accountability, and control mechanisms.

Of course there has been much criticism of Ricardo Semler and Semco. Semler's approach would only be applicable in small businesses, people need management, and need to be controlled and be accountable.

The reality of Semco today makes short shrift of these criticisms. Sales have increased by over 600 percent over the last ten years while profits are up 500 percent. The annual growth rate has been at 24 percent over the past decade and turnover is now over $ 200 million. This is up from $ 4 million when Ricardo Semler took over the company. Employee turnover is very low. Semco is Brazil's most popular employer. There are 2,000 applications on file. There is a turnover rate of less than 1% of the 3,000 employees working for Semco presently.

Ricardo Semler responds to the outside criticism by pointing to the fact that hierarchically led businesses with a strong leader often fail after the leader leaves.He also states that traditional businesses may feel threatened by the Semco way because it means the end for the manager old-style with his many privileges, extremely high salaries, and bonuses.

There are more fine examples of this state-of-the-art value chain approach. One of them is the Belgian company Katoennatie, a transporting company with 3,000 employees, also organized in small autonomous business units. The three examples mentioned in this chapter, Scott Bader, Semco, and Katoennatie could only bloom in their new style because they have had owners who were visionary and really innovative.

CHAPTER 11

Money and interest

"To take interest for money lent is unjust in itself, because this is to sell what does not exist, and this evidently leads to inequality, which is contrary to justice.

Now, money was invented chiefly for the purpose of exchange.

Hence, it is by its very nature unlawful to take payment for the use of money lent, which payment is known as interest."

THOMAS AQUINAS (1247)

Why has interest a devastating effect on the economy, and why do the rich get richer and the poor get poorer through it? And why do the world religions warn against interest?

Let me give you an example to make the impact of interest clear. 150 years ago your great grandfather deposited $ 100 in a savings account at an interest of 5%. Now the savings have a value of $ 150,797, which is $ 150,697 more than the amount laid in, due to interest. Now let us assume that 250 years ago another distant forefather deposited $ 100 also at 5% interest. The present value of this saving is $ 19,830,094, due to 250 years interest added. If the amount had been deposited 500 years ago its present value would be unimaginable high: $ 3,932,326,182,722, due to 500 years interest added. Interest has apparently an exponential effect, the longer the period the disproportionally higher the amount.

In nature all exponential biological processes lead to extinguishment. For example, active cancer cells that divide exponentially destroy all healthy cells and lead in the end to the death of the complete organism. Interest is comparable to the cancer process. In the beginning it slowly destroys an organism, and in the end attacks the bodily or economic 'organism' at a raging speed. Therefore, basically, interest is the major cause of repeated crises.

The money value of GDP is in the end what a country can afford to pay. The bigger the debt governments, businesses, and private households altogether have, the higher the interest claim on the countries' GDP. The German academic Prof. Dr. Margrit Kennedy has done research on the role and influence of interest on the German economy. She reports as follows about her findings:

> What most people don't understand is that every price we pay includes a certain amount of interest. The exact proportion varies according to the capital versus the labor, maintenance, administra-

tive and other costs of the goods and services we buy. This ranges from a 12 % interest component for garbage collection, (because here the share of capital costs is relatively low and the share of physical labor is particularly high) to 38% for drinking water and up to 77% in the rent for public housing (over 100 years, which is the time houses in Germany mostly last). **On the average we pay about 40% interest in all the prices of our goods and services.** In medieval times people paid 'the tenth' of their income or produce to the feudal landlord. In this respect they were better off than we are nowadays.

SOURCE: READING 'WHY DO WE NEED MONETARY INNOVATION'

It is clear that private households bear the biggest interest burden. Rent, mortgage interest, public services, car finance to mention some examples. Also small and medium-sized companies are important payers of interest because they are generally reliant on bank loans. This is more than the larger companies as they are able to attract share capital.

Who are the beneficiaries of interest payments?

Kennedy says on this issue:

Since everyone has to pay interest when borrowing money and receives interest for savings, we are all equally well off within the present money system. On the contrary, there are indeed huge differences as to who profits and who pays in this system. Comparing the interest payments and income from interest in ten equal parts of 2.5 million households in Germany, this figure shows that 80% of the population pay almost twice as much as they receive, 10% receive slightly more than they pay, and the remaining 10% receive more than twice as much interest as they pay, that is the share the first 80% lose. This illustrates one of the least understood reasons why the rich get richer and the poor get poorer. In Germany, in the year 2004, this amounted to a transfer of about € 1 billion ! every day from those who work for their money to those can make their 'money work for them'. In other words, in our monetary system we allow the operation of a hidden redistribution mechanism which continually transfers money from the large majority to a small minority, creating a social polarization which over time will undermine any democracy.

SOURCE: READING 'WHY DO WE NEED MONETARY INNOVATION'

This is shocking information when combined with the nature of interest. And if one realizes that the situation is still mild compared to that in the U.S. where 5% of the population has more income and capital than the remaining 95%, the role of interest becomes quite clear. It is a mechanism that enslaves the vast majority of the world population to a very small minority.

The claims on value added by the real economy are many. Debtholders, shareholders, governments, businesses and private households compete for their shares. In this game, debtholders (banks) and shareholders are on the winning side. Governments impose many types of taxes on their citizens in order to get their share. Income taxes, value added taxes, duties, local taxes, real estate taxes, wealth taxes; governments are really very creative in skimming the value added by their citizens. Of course also private households need their share. The free consumable income is generally low, due to the pressure on it from taxes, interest, and down payments of debts. To be able to do all things and buy all products suggested by the marketers there is continuous need of more income. Consequently, due to all those claims, the economy needs to produce more and more products, services (such as transports), raw materials, oil and gas etc. The earth with its animal, vegetable and mineral resources, people, cultures, and environment is constantly exploited. The exhaustion of all our natural and human resources goes in a terrible speed. Think for example of the tropic woods, oil, gas, iron, copper, fish and many more. This exploitation comes along with an incredible inefficient use of resources, for example, oil-spills, toxins through mining of minerals, destruction of wild life by cutting wood on a large scale, etc.. Even worse, bio-diversity is sacrificed in the pursuit of more money. Bio-diversity is at the basis of a healthy nature. The major deficiency and cause of all this trouble is the crippled idea that money can make money.

Interest could never have played this role if we had not submitted ourselves collectively to the idea that money has value in itself. In fact, not the ones that consciously or unconsciously enslave us are crazy. We are the fools. We allow a small minority of the world population to skim the value we create through our efforts continuously. In this context I would like to remind you of the fact that money is created out of thin air by banks. Printing a piece of paper (with toxic ink), creates paper money, or by simply pressing the button (digital money). There is no coverage of that money by precious metals or any other valuable commodities. If you sign a loan contract, and the bank pushes the button, digital money is created and debited to your account. The only thing banks have to take care of is that the ratio between money created and money held in cash is within the range stipulated by their central bank. This ratio or leverage is very high, so there is a wide playing field for banks.

The massive amounts of debt that are created in this way become a continuously increasing burden for governments, businesses and private households. In the U.S. the total debt of governments, businesses, and private households together amounted to $ 57 trillion in April 2010 (source: America's total debt report). That means that the vast majority is massively in debt to a small minority. It also means that, knowing that the gross domestic product (=sum of the value of all products and services in the U.S.) was $ 14.4 trillion in 2009 (source: CIA fact book); the total debt is nearly 4 times bigger than America's GDP. In other countries all over the world the situation is no different: the citizens of the European Union have a total private debt of $ 20.9 trillion (C.I.A. fact book), for a big part caused by the housing bubble in many EU countries. The people of Japan have a total private debt of $ 9.6 trillion (C.I.A. fact book). Even in China there is developing a schism between a vast majority of have-nots in debt to a small minority of increasingly extremely rich, with a growth of 130 billionaires per year.

If you add up all debts the world population has, the sum of it is an immense amount. According to Kennedy the interest over this amount moves constantly in the direction of the very small minority that gets richer with trillions of money each year. But similar to China and the U.S. who are tied through the extremely high debt from the U.S. to China, the small minority is tied to the vast majority too.

Imagine that one day the have-not majority of people were to awake and simply would not acknowledge their debts anymore. (Similar to the earlier mentioned Jubilee year (cf: Chapter 4), however then proclaimed by the people themselves, and not by their authorities). *Money, created out of thin air would go back to thin air!* That would be great, wouldn't it? The only major drawback, however, is that the vast majority, unfortunately, still believes in the rightfulness of the present money system, and that the victims of that system will defend it with their lives. This is also due to the fact that there is a mechanism to cover up the problem, and that is inflation. Inflation is generated by creating more money than necessary if it were in line with the increase (or decrease) of the GDP. The result of this is a devaluation of money. For example, between 1950 and 2001 the Deutschmark lost **80%** of its value, due to inflation (Kennedy). A loaf of bread for example costing 0.4 DMark in 1950, cost 2 DMark in 2001, due to inflation. This devaluation helps those who are in debt, because it can be paid off more easily. Governments, when heavily in debt, have an interest in inflation. Because while the amount of debt remains the same, prices and incomes are up, thus generating more tax income. So, inflation could

be considered as the natural ally of governments in debt. The haves on the other hand, do not like inflation, because the money value of their property declines through it. That is why governments that serve the interests of the haves are inclined to somehow arrange adjustments to this loss.

Central Banks are at the basis of money creation. They can induce a widening or reduction of the money supply, that is, insofar as they are in control, because the creation of derivatives (options, swaps, futures, etc.) is something these central banks find hard to manage. That hard, that the exact size of it (M3 in the financial terminology), is not published anymore by for example the FED. (the total amount of derivates is said to be more than 50 times the Worlds GDP, according to LEAP institute).

When should, according to the monetary theory, the money supply be enlarged? Primarily in times when the economy needs to be stimulated, and investments are necessary to create new opportunities. In these peculiar times, however, the massive new money creation does not lead to a solid recovery of the economy. Investment levels remain low.

Why then do the financial authorities go on creating more money? Ben Bernanke, chairman of the U.S. FED, for example announced a new injection of a trillion dollars in September 2010. The answer might be that the financial authorities do not have another choice. Reducing the money supply would imply an immediate collapse. Keeping the money supply on the same level means a status quo or worse deflation, which means that the burden of the immense debt becomes even bigger because the working of deflation is inversed to that of inflation. However, also new injections of money do not work because the present system is not able to lead the money flow to those places where they will be invested in really useful projects, other than in the 'business as usual' (for the bigger part financial transactions). There is of course also an awareness in the financial world of the systemic deficiencies of the money system, and the risks involved. More and more financial authorities speak of a necessary reform. Take, for example, this fragment of a speech by Ben Bernanke, addressed to the Financial Stability Board:

> Capital regulations require that banks' capital ratios meet or exceed fixed minimum standards for the bank to be considered safe and sound by regulators. Because banks typically find raising capital to be difficult in economic downturns or periods of financial stress, their best means of boosting their regulatory capital ratios during difficult periods may be to reduce new lending, perhaps more so than is justified by the credit environment. We should review capital regulations to ensure that they are appropriately forward-looking, and that capital is allowed to serve its intended role as a buffer – **one built up during good times and drawn down during**

> **bad times in a manner consistent with safety and soundness.** In the area of prudential supervision, we should also ensure that bank examiners appropriately balance the need for caution and the benefits of maintaining profitable lending relationships when evaluating bank loan policies.

Bernanke, advocates a more flexible approach, by building up capital buffers in good times and allowing them to be swallowed up in bad times. However, the present financial system with all its shortcomings remains in tact, despite of the reforms financial authorities and governments have in mind. Reforming is just fighting symptoms. The only real solution would be a complete renovation or rebuilding of the money system based on a completely different view on money than we have had for ages.

Bernard Lietaer (Reading: *The future of money in our society*, 8 June 2010) advocates a balance between structure and efficiency on the one side and diversity and interconnectivity on the other. In his view, too much focus on structure and efficiency leads to brittleness and in the end collapse of the system. Diversity and interconnectivity should remain functional. If not, it will ultimately lead to chaos. Lietaer supports diversity combined with interconnectivity as basic values in a new monetary system, because they will grant it more resilience. However, Lietaer indicates that cooperation and coordination are essential to make it work. It is similar to bio-diversity. Plants, trees, animals, and insects can provide a healthy biotope providing that there is interconnectivity and there are no creatures in the system that dominate the others or just live for themselves excluding the rest.

Are banking institutes superfluous in a new financial structure? I don't think so, because banks also may add real economic value. Think, for instance, of the organisation of domestic and international payments, their ability to balance risks on loans requested by private households and businesses and make the right decisions about granting loans or not, and the management of business accounts. The big difference, however, will be their business model. This would no longer be based on earning interest and creating shareholder value.

In a really new monetary system governments create debt free money, as the American Colonies did in the 18th century, before they were blocked by the Currency Act, as described in Chapter 4. Banks would no longer be entitled to create (debt) money. Instead, banks would be given the task to distribute the money in a way that serves prosperity and a healthy development of the economy, and of course, not by granting loans to businesses and private households that are not eligible. How could banks generate revenue? Well, just like all other service industries, by asking for fees based on the services rendered. In that case the bills presented to their clients would also be better understood, because they should be in line with the value delivered by banks.

Interest, particularly compounded interest, or usury is something more world religions have warned against. Islamic banking for example is becoming increasingly popular. This type of banking does not calculate interest on loans.

> Islamic banking refers to a system of banking or banking activity that is consistent with the principles of Islamic law (Sharia) and its practical application through the development of Islamic economy. Sharia prohibits the payment or acceptance of interest fees for the lending and accepting of money respectively, (riba, ususry) for specific terms, as well as investing in businesses that provide goods or services considered contrary to its principles (Haraam, forbidden). While these principles were used as the basis for a flourishing economy in earlier times, it is only in the late 20th century that a number of Islamic banks were formed to apply these principles to private or semi-private commercial institutions within the Muslim community.
>
> **SOURCE:** WIKIPEDIA

In its pure application, Islamic banking could make an end to inflation, and the development of massive debts. However, for many people Islamic banking is not an option as they do not share the Muslim faith.

Therefore we have to look for a solution that is free from any belief and 'ism'. It would help if there were an organisation that is already bringing this idea into practice. And actually there is. It is the Swedish JAK Medlemsbank, active as a bank with a banking license as from 1997. This bank does not calculate interest on loans and does not pay interest on savings either. Members of this cooperative bank pay a subscription fee of Swedish Crowns (SEK) 200 (Eur. 21.70) per year. For this fee the members receive points. Also they receive points for the savings deposited in JAK Bank. These points can be used if the member needs a loan from the JAK Bank.

An example may clarify how it works:
An interest free loan of SEK 100,000, will be repaid in 10 years in monthly installments of SEK 833.33. Furthermore, there is a fee totaling SEK 12,960, payable in monthly installments of SEK 108. This appears to be a big amount. However, compared to a regular loan it is not much. For example, at 7% interest per year the borrower pays SEK 35,000 interest over 10 years + an amount for provision + a yearly amount for credit costs. This is a big difference to the advantage of the JAK Bank system. Another monthly payment is the compulsive deposit in a savings account, during 10 years. If the borrower has no points, it is an amount of SEK 833.33 per month, therefore the more points available the lower the compulsory savings deposits. If, for example, the client would have saved SEK 1,500 during 48 months before borrowing SEK 100,000, the compulsory savings amount per month would be not SEK 833.33 but SEK 590.

This arrangement has been made by the JAK Bank to have a buffer in case the borrower defaults. At the end of year 10 the savings deposit is free to be withdrawn by the client.

How successful is the JAK Medlemsbank in their present business model? In 2010 there were 38,000 members, contributing SEK 7.6 million per year. The total volume of money borrowed and saved is SEK 2 billion. The total revenue was in 2009 SEK 26 million, and total expenses SEK 28 million. The revenue was thus too low to cover the costs. Over the past five years JAK Bank suffered four years of losses, and made profit in just one year. Although they are operating on a low cost basis, the expenses are apparently too high for the scale of operations. Recently they have started to move in the direction of an internet bank, aiming to reduce costs.

It is not easy for an ideal-driven organization like the JAK Bank to survive in a world in which interest is completely embedded. One has to have a clear idea about what interest does to the earth, environment, people, and world economy. Otherwise, depositing savings at 0% would be foolish, because your money will not just bring no return, it will even decline in value through inflation. That is why the JAK Bank pays much attention to informing people. The most important reasons for interest-free banking they communicate are:

- Interest destabilizes the economy
- Interest is the main reason for inflation
- Interest contributes to unemployment, inflation and exhaustion of natural resources
- Interest causes concentration of money by a small minority of people.

These arguments are very similar to those I have discussed in this chapter. It is clear that it is hard to survive for an organisation like JAK Bank in a world that appears to be not yet ready for it. Nevertheless, the effort deserves lots of respect, because it is a forerunner of a better world.

If we relied on the findings of Prof. Dr. Margrit Kennedy, the pressure on the value created by the real economy would lessen by 40%

in a interest free economy. Prices of goods and services could drop at that percentage. There would be no more devaluation of the value of money through inflation, considerably lower taxes, stable values of the currencies, and no more crises. If only we were able to say goodbye to a system that has caused us lots of misery for centuries.

CHAPTER 12

Ending the Global Casino?

In economics the factors of production are land, labour, and capital.
I agree with that. However, instead of production I say Wealth, instead of land I speak of Planet and instead of labour I prefer People.
Planet, People, and Capital are the sources of Wealth, and in this
sequence, Capital last.

SATISH KUMAR, 30 SEPTEMBER 2010 NEW FINANCIAL FORUM, THE HAGUE

The World is deep in debt. Private debts of the U.K. (households + businesses) the U.S., and the Eurozone together amount to an unimaginable $ 100 trillion plus. Government debts of the U.K., U.S., and Eurozone add another $ 25 trillion plus. Assuming that the interest rate is 4%, an amount of at least $ 5 trillion is due each year. This amount is paid to the debtholders. A very small minority is net debtholder, as pointed out in Chapter 11. So a considerable part of this

$ 5 trillion interest is received by those net debt-holders. As debts are increasing year by year with large amounts, there is a continuous shift of increasing amounts of money from the vast majority of people to a very small minority.

As the total amount of debt is 4 to 5 times bigger than the total GDP of the eurozone, U.S., and U.K. together, one can imagine that it needs more - rigorously economizing - generations to get out of this debt, which is impossible in a financial system that is based on money as debt. For that reason one does not have to be a learned specialist with great vision to predict the collapse of this system. Governments, businesses, and private households are dependent on the debtholders. In fact their economic fate is in the hands of these creditors. To governments the biggest 'asset' they have are the countries' citizens. Their potential to produce added value is the best collateral they can offer to the debtholders. Taxation is the way to skim the value produced by citizens, especially income tax, which is the biggest source of revenues. Together with premiums for national insurance and council tax a considerable part of the gross wages is claimed by so-called direct taxes in countries such as the U.K. (by average 37.5%) and The Netherlands (by average 40%). Apart from direct taxes governments also have indirect taxes as a means to increase revenues. For example value added taxes (VAT), 10-11% of the sales price is for the good of the country. In the Netherlands VAT is paid on an average of 10.1% of the personal income, and in the U.K. 11% (£ 81 billion in 2009). By the way, businesses do not pay VAT. They just cash it on behalf of the Treasury.

Another instrument to increase government's revenue is excise duties. Tobacco, spirits, wine, beer, fuel, air passages and vehicles added £ 53 billion to the U.K.'s HM Treasury in 2009. On average 6.5% of the U.K. citizen's income is claimed by excise duties, and in The Netherlands 5.1%, which in fact levels the difference in direct taxes between the U.K. and The Netherlands. Indirect taxes push up prices, and direct taxes take away a part of the income. If governments need to cover their deficits, and they need to maintain purchasing power, the way to do this is to increase VAT, excise duties, energy and property tax (vehicles, houses, boats, etc.). The consequence of this is increasing prices. Governments are main triggers of inflation. In Chapter 11 I have explained why inflation is convenient to them.

Of course governments such as the U.K.'s and the Dutch' one spend a lot on pensions, health care, education, and welfare. In the U.K. this was £ 390 billion in 2009, which was 71% of the total tax revenues in that year. An increasing part of the expenditure, however, is claimed by 'servicing the national debt', particularly when repayments are not be financed by new debt anymore. Furthermore, the huge amounts spent on welfare and health care could be reduced considerably and prices would be reduced if people's incomes were not be loaded that heavily with tax. Private incomes are burdened by taxes, direct and indirect, insurance premiums, and also by interest payments and debt repayments. Governments, banks, and insurance companies claim the bigger part of our incomes. In The Netherlands this is an incredibly high **72.5%** (direct taxes and premiums 47.3%, indirect taxes 15.2%, and –on average- 10%- interest) And if the indirect interest, Kennedy has written about, is included, our incomes are for an even bigger part taken away by direct and indirect taxes plus direct and indirect interest. The situation in The Netherlands is not exceptional; the main difference is by means of what type of tax the countries treasury is filled. In Germany the V.A.T. revenue is relatively high, and the Income Tax revenue relatively low. Germany is very kind to its rich. This small example proves that:

Klaus B. is a millionaire. His income is generated by his capital of € 5 million. Klaus pays just € 2,300 tax. Dagmar and Jurgen D. are employees and have three sons. They pay on their combined income € 16,000 tax, which is seven times more than that of the millionaire.

SOURCE: HTTP://WWW.3SAT.DE/PAGE/?SOURCE=/ARD/SENDUNG/146383/INDEX.HTML-

SOURCES USED FOR THE CALCULATION OF TAX BURDEN: WWW.HM-TREASURY.GOV.UK ,
WWW.MINFIN.NL , WWW.CBS.NL, WWW.DEBTBOMBSHELL.COM , WWW.WIKIPEDIA.CO.UK,
WWW.THISISMONEY.CO.UK

The super-rich have their loopholes to avoid taxes. In June 2007 in an article in the *Evening Standard* their tax behaviour was analysed:

Only a fraction of Britain's super-rich are paying income tax.

At least 400 UK-based individuals earn, or are capable of making, £10m a year. But only 65 paid income tax, according to the latest figures obtained under the Freedom of Information Act. The rest use a battery of sophisticated but legal techniques to avoid paying. It is not known exactly how much money is being lost to the taxpayer in this way but analysis by the Standard suggests it could be as much as £2bn a year. Treasury figures obtained by the Standard show that 65 people who filed a tax return in 2004-05 declared a taxable income of £ 10m or more. But, according to the Sunday Times Rich List, there are more than 350 people in Britain with a fortune of at least £200m-enough to generate a return of £10m-a year through **dividends**, interest, rents and profits. Furthermore, an estimated 30 City traders earn at least £10m, as do 30 company directors, including top hedge fund managers, private equity executives and industrialists such as vacuum cleaner tycoon Sir James Dyson. Latest figures show that Britons earning more than £1m a year paid a total of £4.6 bn in tax in 2004-05, a tax rate of 35.9%. But it appears most of that was paid by the 'poor rich' who earn just over seven figures.

The top 1,000 richest people in Britain are worth a combined £360bn, suggesting annual earnings of around £18 bn. If the same average tax rate was applied to these earnings, the top 1,000 people alone would be paying £6.5bn in tax, one-and-a-half times Britain's overseas aid budget. Although the biggest single tax loophole, non-domicile status, is under review by the Treasury, the Government under Tony Blair has been reluctant to order a clampdown for fear of damaging the City and the economy. Other loopholes have been closed only for another to open up.

The issue has been highlighted by the row over the breaks enjoyed by senior private equity partners, who can reduce the tax they pay on profits from selling companies to 10% or even less. The issue has split the industry, with figures such as Sir Ronald, who is worth an estimated £260m, saying his colleagues should pay more tax and executives such as Guy Hands of Terra Firma saying they take far greater risks than other businessmen and so should enjoy the breaks.

One senior accountant involved in designing tax avoidance schemes said: 'A lot of these individuals would rather keep the money and direct it towards the issues that affect them. 'They feel that if they give it to the Government it will be spent on stuff that is not applicable to them or they don't agree with.'

By using the tax break called business asset taper relief, private equity executives are estimated to have avoided paying as much as £1 bn in personal tax over the past quarter of a century. Dominic Murphy of Kohlberg Kravis Roberts and Co - which recently took over Boots, Damon Buffini of Pemira and Robert Easton, the managing director of the Carlyle Group, were all asked by MPs how much they paid in capital gains. 'The rich and well-advised exploit loopholes and end up paying 10% tax rather than 40%. Non-domiciles taking advantage of offshore trusts avoid **Capital Gains Tax**, and people avoid stamp duty by registering their house as being owned by a company. The current system is creating a corrosive sense of unfairness.'

A poor man's guide to the loopholes:

NON-DOMICILE STATUS – Dates back to the 18th century and was designed to persuade British colonists to settle in far-flung corners of the Empire. Now it is exploited by foreign billionaires who can legally base themselves in Britain but pay no tax on their overseas earnings. In the 2004/05 tax year, 112,000 individuals claimed non-domicile status.

NON-RESIDENT STATUS – British citizens can escape UK tax if they do not spend an average of more than 90 days a year in Britain over four years. Until last year, days spent travelling did not count, so tax exiles would arrive on Monday morning and leave on Wednesday evening, yet claim to have spent only one day here. This anomaly has now been closed.

OFFSHORE TRUSTS – British members of the super-rich who live here can minimise their tax bill through trusts in tax havens such as the Channel Islands or British Virgin Islands. If the assets owned by the trust are not held in the name of the individual and any income or capital gains is not returned to Britain, these are usually beyond the reach of the taxman.

SOURCE: EVENING STANDARD, 21 JUNE 2007

The article in the *Evening Standard* shows just a glimpse of the immense wealth in the hands of the super-rich, hidden from the eyes of the Treasury. If you think that this matter has been solved, here is a very recent fragment out of an article in the *Financial Times*:

All higher-rate taxpayers are to be subject to increased scrutiny by the Revenue & Customs under a "ruthless" crackdown on "morally indefensible" tax avoidance and evasion.

The measures, announced by Danny Alexander, Treasury chief secretary, are designed to recoup up to £7bn ($11bn) from 2014-15, following a £900m cumulative investment in enforcement teams. The funding will expand the "high net worth unit". Aides said the number of individuals scrutinised by the team would increase from about 5,000 to encompass all 150,000 individuals paying the 50p rate of tax. A dedicated team will be created to catch those "hiding money" offshore, according to aides. The fund will also underwrite efforts to clamp down on organised crime, smuggling and value added tax fraud. The government aims to quintuple criminal prosecutions for tax offences.

SOURCE: FINANCIAL TIMES, 19 SEPTEMBER 2010

Our greed is their grip on us. Greed? Yes, for example the top 0.1% earners and tax payers in the U.K. are small in numbers, just 42,000 people. They earn on average £ 786,000 per year, *which is more than 10% of all income in the U.K.* They pay, also on average £ 286,000 tax, leaving them 'just' net £ 500,000, which is actually 29 times more than the on average net £ 18,000 the lower 90% of the British taxpayers earn. Yet the top 0.1% earners-taxpayers complain about the amount of tax they have to pay, and consider leaving the country if the highest tax bracket would be raised to 50%. (Source: Institute for fiscal studies, January 2008) This example is of course also applicable to the U.S., Germany, France, etc.

The 'poor' rich complain about the tax burden on their incomes. The four hundred people mentioned in the article in the Evening Standard still have names. Above them are the unknown super-rich, that are not under the jurisdiction of any government. These super-rich can afford expensive international tax advisors to show them the ways to the loopholes in the tax system. The treasury of the countries that host the super-rich can only guess how much tax revenue they actually miss. The wealth of the super-rich is out of reach for them, leaving the burden described earlier to the vast majority.

In the 18th century modern banking developed. Central banks, in private hands were established. Based on a fractional reserve in gold, the bankers created money out of thin air and lent it to governments. Governments went heavily in debt with the bankers, especially through the many wars that were fought. The owners of these banks grew incredibly rich. Incredibly rich and incredibly powerful. The bankers could make and break countries, economies, royal dynasties, dictators, whatever suited them best in their insatiable hunger for money and power. This financial elite has no name these days, because they can afford all the loopholes the world can offer. They have turned the world into a global casino. In this casino there are just a few winners, and for the rest just losers, seen from the viewpoint of 'who is in debt' and 'who has to pay the bill'. If debts become too high, the financial elite will not give us relief like in the old days, when there was the Jubelee year. No, like true casino bosses all 'players' are deprived of their assets if their debts become too massive to be repaid. And that is exactly what is going to happen. If you still have your doubts, read this analysis made by the Global Research Institute (Canada) of the proclamation of 'Basel III', by the BIS Bank;

THE PROBLEM

The major global banks are all **under-capitalised** and this was all too apparent when Lehman Bros. collapsed. Banks were borrowing so much and so recklessly to play at the global casino that when the bets went sour, they were staring at a black-hole in the \$trillions. In fact the banks are all insolvent.

The problem was compounded when the central bankers (all are corrupt without exception) and regulators turned a blind eye to how bankers defined what constituted "capital" so as to circumvent the need to maintain the capital ratio.

THE BASEL III SOLUTION

At its 12 September 2010 meeting, the Group of Governors and Heads of Supervision, the oversight body of the Basel Committee on Banking Supervision, announced a substantial strengthening of existing capital requirements and fully endorsed the agreements it reached on 26 July 2010. These capital reforms, together with the introduction of a global liquidity standard, deliver on the core of the global financial reform agenda and will be presented to the Seoul G20 Leaders summit in November. The Committee's package of reforms will increase the minimum common equity requirement from 2% to 4.5%. In addition, banks will be required to hold a capital conservation buffer of 2.5% to withstand future periods of stress bringing the total common equity requirements to 7%.

THE LOOPHOLE & ADMISSION OF INSOLVENCY

Since the onset of the crisis, banks have already undertaken substantial efforts to raise their capital levels. However, preliminary results of the Basel Committee's comprehensive quantitative impact study show that as of the end of 2009, large banks will need, in the aggregate, a significant amount of additional capital to meet these new requirements. Smaller banks, which are particularly important for lending to the SME sector, for the most part already meet these higher standards.

The Governors and Heads of Supervision also agreed on transitional arrangements for implementing the new standards. These will help ensure that the banking sector can meet the higher capital standards through reasonable earnings retention and capital raising, while still supporting lending to the economy.

LIFE SUPPORT

The central bankers cannot have the cake and eat it as well. In trying to shore up public confidence in banks with the introduction of Basel III, they have inadvertently let the cat out of the bag because the banks are all insolvent. Additionally, whatever reserves that have been accumulated are insufficient to stimulate further lending, because the banks have reached their limits under the fractional reserve system. This is the reason for the contraction of credit and not as one commentator has postulated that Basel III would "contract credit".

Two burdens are weighing down on the banks:
1) inadequate capital to meet liabilities (borrowings); and
2) inadequate reserves under fractional reserve banking.

This is a big mess!

THE CONFIDENCE GAME

At this moment, I cannot give a precise time-line as to how long the FED and the global central banks can prolong the confidence game, hoodwinking the public and sovereign creditors that all is well. When confidence in banks evaporates for whatever reasons, the consequences will be ugly and there will be massive social up-heavals across the globe. The first indication that the game is up is when US treasuries are increasingly purchased by the FED to make up for the shortfalls by foreign creditors and to finance the ballooning US deficits.

All of a sudden, some entities may start to get real nervous and unload the treasuries, and the FED steps in to shore up treasuries. Then, the tipping point is reached and Hell breaks loose!
China is also part of this confidence game.

But, contrary to IMF and other renowned economists who are betting on China's and Asia's so-called economic strengths, I take the view that when US treasuries collapse, **faith in all fiat monies will likewise evaporate and there will be massive capital flight to commodities, especially gold, silver and oil.**

Asian stock markets will be devastated and there will be volatile gyrations in currency values. Therefore, it is utter lunacy and reck-lessness for the Malaysian central bank (Bank Negara) and the government to even consider allowing the ringgit to be traded. When confidence in dollar assets vaporises, China will be caught right in the middle. The third and final phase of the Global Financial Tsunami will devastate Asian economies and with it, the greatest depression in history will ensue.

Time Line? Between now and anytime in 2011. At the latest, 2012.

SOURCE: WWW.GLOBALRESEARCH.CA BASEL III, 20 SEPTEMBER 2010 (FRAGMENTS)

In my opinion Basel III will just speed-up the events predicted by the Global Research Institute. All banks are, as they correctly state, insolvent. Their ability to absorb losses is far too low. And there are still a lot of toxic assets on the balance sheets (or hidden through constructs) of all major banks. Therefore the solvency may come more under pressure. If the confidence game is over, the bosses will close the casino, leaving all players in disaster.

What are sure signals for the closure of the global casino?
- Increasing debts,
- Increasing unemployment,
- Insolvencies, both with private households and businesses,
- Bankruptcies,
- Governments without success desperately trying to get their budgets in balance by raising more taxes and cutting expenses,
- Increasing prices and decreasing purchasing power through accelerating inflation.

Only the last signal is not obvious yet. Inflation is –officially – kept low. This is done by changing the package of goods and services that are the statistical basis for measuring inflation. And by keeping the interest on savings low. Lower than the real devaluation of money. All people that cut their personal spending and put more savings in the bank help unwillingly to keep the inflation low. At the same time their money loses value, because the devaluation of money goes faster than the interest accrued.

At the brink of crisis in the past, people who recognized the signals, bought gold and silver for their money. Again, especially when the confidence game is over, inflation is booming and the value of money begins to devaluate in a dizzying speed, one could consider buying gold, silver, or raw materials. Maybe, if the Casino bosses re-open for a new game those precious metals and raw materials have value then. However, the chance that one does not get the value in new money that has been invested in old money is not unthinkable. Furthermore, by doing so one helps to re-establish the old system with the same bosses. The only difference is another story told to make us believe that the world will be better, and all people all over the world will be free and happy. Forget it! The minds of those who set up the new game will not have changed at all! Even worse, because those who are not obedient might be set aside as persona non grata. Because a centrally lead system cannot accept opposition.

How can we stop this casino? By refurnishing and giving it a sustainable and green image? The habits will not change. Provoking our greed and promoting ambition, going for the first prize, failing all others will still be the game. The bonus culture that has been resumed after the last crisis proves it. How can we stop the casino then? Yes, by refusing to play the game anymore. By coming alive to the fact that the casino bosses are dependent on us, and we not on them. We are able to create a new economy. We can leave the Mickey Mouse money to the casino and we can demand that our governments bring debt-free money into circulation.

We do not need banks, at least not in their present shape. You can decide where your money will be invested in, no longer leaving this to banks that just go for shareholder value. You can invest in people. Especially those who are down-to-earth, integer, have bright minds and are willing to put their energy into creating a really better world. You might invest your money into small and medium-sized companies that are innovative, and led by honest people. Is that risky? That is what bankers will tell you. But this is not true. One might invest in people who contribute to the solution of the pollution of the earth, develop sustainable energy that really helps to cover the growing need for energy, solutions for the food problem and many more. The return on investment will come slowly. There will not be short term profits. But in the longer term the return will not only be material, it will also bring a lot of happiness. No more shareholder value, no more priority given to financial return on investment but on societal return on investment.

Ending the Global Casino, leaving their bosses unemployed instead of us, will make way for a truly better world. In this book I have given more examples of people, organisations, movements that are seriously working toward bringing about a new economy, with money in a supporting instead of a leading role. I have mentioned a few; Bader, Semler, Transition Towns, BerkShares, JAK Bank and WIR Bank. But there are many truly inspiring initiatives all over the world. The choice is yours.

Business Angels and Business Dragons

An angel investor or angel (also known as a business angel or informal investor) is an affluent individual who provides capital for a business start-up, usually in exchange for convertible debt or ownership equity. A small but increasing number of angel investors organize themselves into angel groups or angel networks to share research and pool their investment capital.

Angel investments bear extremely high risk and are usually subject to dilution from future investment rounds. As such, they require a very high return on investment. Because a large percentage of angel investments are lost completely when early stage companies fail, professional angel investors seek investments that have the potential to return at least 10 or more times their original investment within 5 years, through a defined exit strategy, such as plans for an initial public offering or an acquisition. Current 'best practices' suggest that angels might do better setting their sights even higher, looking for companies that will have at least the potential to provide a 20x-30x return over a five- to seven-year holding period. After taking into account the need to cover failed investments and the multi-year holding time for even the successful ones, however, the actual effective internal rate of return for a typical successful portfolio of angel investments is, in reality, typically as 'low' as 20-30%. While the investor's need for high rates of return on any given investment can thus make angel financing an expensive source of funds, cheaper sources of capital, such as bank financing, are usually not available for most early-stage ventures, which may be too small or young to qualify for traditional loans.

SOURCE: WIKIPEDIA

Summarized, business angels or informal investors ask a lot of money in return for the risk taken to lend money to a starting business. If they buy shares in the business, the idea is to sell them a few years later for a much higher price. The reason for business angels to do that, is that it is said that they lose a lot of money due to all the failing businesses where they have invested in. In many countries business angel networks have developed over the past few years, encourages by their governments. An example of such a Business Angel Network can be found in Australia. This network lists the offers made by Angel Investors on internet: http://www.businessangels.com.au/angels.php. Investors looking for starting sustainable and innovating businesses are exceptional on that list. The majority looks for companies in industries they have experience in, and do not want to leave their familiar ways.

Business Angels are generally not interested in financing the day-to-day business activities (working capital). That is why they are out of reach for the majority of SMEs, as the major problem of them is lack of cash to finance the normal business activities. Many of the SME entrepreneurs cannot even think about investing in new green technologies, as the focus is on surviving and keeping the cash flow going.

The idea that the failure these days of many SMEs can be considered as a healthy shake out of outdated entrepreneurs and businesses is, to put it mildly, short-sighted. There are many experienced entrepreneurs who would be willing and are capable to innovate the business, if only they could put their energy in this process, and if they would have the capital at their disposal to safeguard the continuity of their companies. To give the necessary support, Business Angels should give more priority to the future health of planet and people as they did until now, and base their decisions more on insight in the human character than on numbers.

More information on Business Angels: http://www.eban.org EBAN serves business angels, business angel networks, seed funds and other early stage investment professionals across Europe.

Nowadays, reality TV enjoys an increasing popularity, for example, The Dragons' Den. This show is broadcasted in many countries all over the world. For new and innovative entrepreneurs seemingly the only road to get the finance they is by exposing themselves in a drag-ons' den show. This comment is on the Canadian version:

> When the banks won't bite on your great idea, try a dose of reality TV. The big plan for economic recovery has turned into something of a dog-and-pony show. Banks that were supposed to be ponying up loan money have been dogging it instead. With tight credit conditions, it sometimes seems the only entrepreneurial money to be found is guarded by another kind of beast entirely: dragons.

> These days if you're a startup seeking a little cash, you may well have to brave the terror of the Dragons' Den. The CBC reality series features a panel of investors – Kevin O'Leary, Arlene Dickinson, Robert Herjavec, Brett Wilson and Jim Treliving – listening to business pitches and deciding whether to invest their own money. "Things are nowhere near as good as the government is making

out," says ringleader O'Leary, calling from the back of a chauffeured car somewhere in Boston. "Large-cap companies worth over a billion are seeing things loosen up now, but nothing is loosening up for small businesses. Dragons' Den is a real option. Where else can you raise $250,000? I'll give it to you if I think I can make money."

SOURCE: HTTP://WWW.BCBUSINESSONLINE.CA

The hopes, efforts, ideals, ingenuity, etc., of young entrepreneurs reduced to show requisites. We can do better, can't we?

The future of planet and people

> One might invest in people who contribute to the solution of the pollution of the earth, develop sustainable energy that really helps to cover the growing need for energy, solutions for the food problem and many more. The return on investment will come slowly. There will not be short term profits. But in the longer term the return will not only be material, it will also bring a lot of happiness. No more shareholder value, no more priority given to financial return on investment but on societal return on investment.
>
> ENDING THE GLOBAL CASINO?, CHAPTER 12

There is the gloomy reality of the monetary system in its present state. On the other hand there are people from all over the world bringing about positive changes. Often in their own company or in the local and regional community they live in. I have mentioned a few examples in my book. Because of their importance for our future they should be brought to the attention of all people who are willing to say goodbye to the global casino, and wish to orientate themselves on a world wherein money is subservient to the economy. An economy that invests in a better future for our planet, its people, and all other living creatures. In the next book I will write about those men and women, initiatives, projects, etc., that are fully involved in realizing this goal.

To give you a taste of what will come in the next book, Mark Anielski (Canada) and Ivo Valkenburg (The Netherlands) tell about their ideals and how they are contributing to a better future for us all.

Building an Economy of Love and Genuine Wealth

Mark Anielski

In my book *The Economics of Happiness: Building Genuine Wealth* (2007, 2009), I present a new road map for developing communities that are founded on well-being, on virtue and ultimately love rather than on materialism. Our economies are in a cancer stage of development with gripped by an unrepayable mountain of debt-based money that can never be repaid despite growing the economy with more production and consumption.

For the ancient Greeks, happiness (*eudamonia*) meant "good spirit" or "well-being of spirit." Happiness related to the condition of one's soul. Aristotle noted that happiness is a sense of well-being resulting from achieving excellence in the fulfillment of one's functions. Thus, happiness is about knowing why you are on the Earth – your vocation or calling. But how many of us actually take the time to listen to God's tender voice calling us to fulfill our purpose for being on this earth? My vision is that of an economy of "genuine wealth"; that means a society where the core values of our hearts are aligned with the measures of our well-being. These well-being indicators will guide our decision-making and budgeting decisions so we can be assured that our actions. Their regular reporting will become the conversation over coffee or tea. In this economy, virtuous actions will be the measure of progress. We will have a new accounting system which takes a regular inventory of the actual conditions well-being of people (physical, mental, spiritual and emotional well-being), the strength of our relationships (social capital) and levels of trust, and the integrity of nature (forests, rivers, the air) that contribute most to our happiness. This new balance sheet for our communities and nations will include 'five capitals' of genuine wealth: human, social, natural, built and even financial capital. In this new economy, money will no longer be the master over humanity but the servant of happiness. Money will be created according to the needs of people and to maintain the flourishing conditions of societies five capital assets. We will invest in areas that threaten our happiness and pose a risk to the well-being of our children and grand children. No longer will we be paying unnecessary interest charges on debt-money, thus rejecting usury, but will learn to become each others bankers. We will learn to trust each other in the spirit of sharing and reciprocity. We will, at last, no longer be worshipping Mammon but the God of Love. Bankers will redeem their own souls by becoming counselors for wise financial stewardship facilitating our happiness. Ultimately, I envision an economy of love characterized not by the current hedonistic spirit of capitalism but by the ethics of trust, relationships, sharing and reciprocity.

I believe the great economist John Maynard Keynes shared my vision when he noted "The day is not far off when the economic problem will take the back seat where it belongs, and the arena of the heart and the head will be occupied or reoccupied, by our real problems – the problems of life and of human relations, of creation and behavior and religion."

In Edmonton, where I live with my wife and two young daughters, we have tried to define our own "good life" by focusing on our genuine wealth and budgeting our time and money accordingly. We examined our core values by getting in touch with "that which makes life worthwhile." We eliminated all of our debts freeing up the most precious of resources – time. We now have to work fewer hours for a high and sustainable quality of life. We have more discretionary income to buy our food and life needs locally, eat organically, and celebrate slow food. We slow down, listen more and pray more. And most importantly, we have more time to spend with our families, our neighbours and in our own personal re-creation. As a result, we are genuinely wealthier. In this new genuine wealth economy which I envision and which many are already helping to construct all over the world (documented in my book), wealth will be defined as the harvest of love. All the relationships of love we have ever had are ours to keep and hold for an eternity. Thus our business plan is rather simple: to be the love that you are and to be the light of love to the World. In other words to live the two great commandments Jesus gave us. When we let go of structure and the lie of scarcity and accept the truth of abundance the real wealth that is there will multiply many times   love pressed down and overflowing. Do we have enough faith and courage to be and act in this truth?

Mark Anielski is President and CEO of Anielski Management Inc. (AMI) located in Edmonton, Alberta. As an economist, he works with communities, businesses and governments to help them assess, measure and manage their genuine wealth – the things that matter most to well-being, quality of life and sustainability. Mark is the author of the best-selling book The Economics of Happiness: Building Genuine Wealth, which was published by New Society Publishers in May 2007, with a second printing in 2009. In 2008 his book won two awards; the gold medal in the category of Consciousness Business Leadership at the Los Angeles Nautilus Book Awards and a bronze medal in the category of Economics at the Axiom Book Awards in New York. In January 2010, it was released in China. The Economics of Happiness provides a roadmap for building a new economy of well-being using Mark's Genuine Wealth model to assess the resilience of human, social, natural, built and financial capital assets.

www.anielski.com

Five Investments for a better future

Ivo Valkenburg

'Love is who we are. Love is all that is and the rest is an illusion' was the most important message of my father who wandered around in the financial world for over forty years. The most significant booster of transformations from ending the global casino to starting the global economy of love will come from those people who choose to become 100% responsible for living a life 'in love with all living creatures'. Looking at those people all around the world, I have come to see at least 5 important investments they make for a better future.

1. INVEST IN SPIRITUALITY ON THE WORKPLACE

We are spiritual beings. We are born to re-discover, embrace and live the full potential of our lives, businesses, and nations. One of the most important jobs to do is to re-connect ourselves for an economy of happiness in a engaging way (body, heart, mind, soul) by empowering our trust, empathy, holism, authenticity and Spirit.

BEST PRACTICE: European Bahá'í Business Forum (www.EBBF.org)
A spiritually inspired non-governmental organisation dedicated to bringing ethical values, personal virtues and moral leadership into our workplaces.

Jeroen Kleijne, freelance journalist
I don't just write
I shed light on important issues

Liong Lie, architect
I don't just design buildings,
I put my heart into each place

Marc Vieten, school leader
I don't just lead a school,
I release human potential

2. MEASURE WHAT YOU VALUE

We live in a environment that is highly affected by what we measure. Using the saying 'measuring = knowing,' plenty of manuals and protocols are striving after 'high output.' Quarterly figures often mean more than people. Let's measure what really counts in live!

BEST PRACTICE: Norway index gauges nature; may bring GDP rethink

An index to judge the state of Norway's nature is a world first that may be a step towards valuing "free" services such as insect pollination or forest growth in a radical shift in economics, officials say. (source: www.uk.reuters.com)

BEST PRACTICE: The Gallup-Healthways Well-Being Index (www.well-beingindex.com)

It's the first-ever daily assessment of U.S. residents' health and well-being. By interviewing at least 1,000 U.S. adults every day, the Well-Being Index provides real-time measurement and insights needed to improve health, increase productivity, and lower health-care costs. Public and private sector leaders use data on life evaluation, physical health, emotional health, healthy behavior, work environment, and basic access to develop and prioritize strategies to help their communities thrive and grow.

3. INVEST YOUR MONEY IN ´HEAVEN ON EARTH´

All over the world more and more people are rising up in love to be inspired by the voice of the heart. This also creates a huge difference in how they want to invest their money. Pension funds, banks, insurance companies and other main financial players increasingly invest their money in a way that provides both financial rewards and offers social and environmental benefits. Return on planet & people will become the new ethical way of dealing with investments. Your money is your daily vote on how you would like to see the world.

BEST PRACTICE: The Government Pension Fund – Norway (www.ftf.no)
This pension fund is one of the biggest funds in the world with only one owner. It is intended to last for many generations. That's why the Norwegian Government has chosen to develop a wide range of ethical principles relating to the investment activities to serve the country, the land, the nature and it's people on the long term.

BEST PRACTICE: Triple Bottom Line Investing (www.tbli.org)
TBLI GROUP™ raises awareness in the financial sector of the benefits of impact investment. It facilitates one of world´s largest networks of thought leaders on sustainability investment.

BEST PRACTICE: Forma Futura www.formafutura.com
Forma Futura Invest Inc. is an independent asset management company. It invest the assets entrusted to them in a way that reflects the clients' personal values, fosters a sustainable quality of life, and earns an adequate return.

4. INVEST IN NEW EDUCATION OF FINANCIAL PROFESSIONALS

The new generation of financial service providers has to be prepared towards ethics, morals, values and developing skills like trust, connectivity, holism and authenticity.

BEST PRACTICE:
The global movement of Financial Life Planning
www.financialdna.com
www.kinderinstitute.com
http://financialawakenings.com
www.moneyquotient.com
www.soulofmoney.org

Financial life planning is the process of (1) helping people focus on the true values and motivations in their lives, (2) determining the goals and objectives they have as they see their lives to develop, and (3) using these values, motivations goals , and objectives to guide the planning process and provide a framework for making choices and decisions in life that have financial and non-financial implications or consequences. Understanding people above numbers.

5. REDESIGN THE WORLD

Be free. Be inspired. Take 100% responsibility yourself.

BEST PRACTICE: The Venus Project (www.thevenusproject.com)
The Venus Project presents a bold, new direction for humanity that entails nothing less than the total redesign of our culture.

BEST PRACTICE: Global Leadership Academy (www.globalleaders academy.com)
The Global Leadership Academy (GLA) is a global network of leaders in business and society. Individuals at the top of 'their' tree who

are committed to creating sustainable wellbeing for themselves, for their organisations and for the wider planet.

BEST PRACTICE: Solari (www.solari.com)
Solari believes that preserving and building personal and family wealth reduces risk and promotes freedom and community wealth broadly

Ivo Valkenburg is the founder and managing director of Spirit in Finance. He was born and raised in a family of financial service providers in search of Spirit. All things connected to finance, authenticity and spirituality are inseparable parts of my character. To him Spirit comes down to infinite love, inspiration and freedom.

'How often do we perceive Spirit in our work? And in all our comings and goings for that matter? How do we re-discover, embrace and live the full potential of our lives, businesses, and nations?'

His work doesn't stop at just helping people answer these questions, He is in a very practical and engaging way re-connecting people to an economy of happiness (body, heart, mind, soul), by empowering trust, empathy, holism, authenticity and Spirit. I am a highly versatile person, and not easy to characterise. Above all he is inspired by the Spirit. He dedicates his enthusiasm to raise the inner voice and beauty in people and organisations. Furthermore, he is the author of "Spirit in Finance, Let your light shine in the world of money and matter". My –not yet from Dutch translated - book was published in October 2009.The goal of his company Spirit in Finance is to change the slant of the financial world. He genuinely wants to help people to think differently about themselves and to integrate spirituality and a better balance in their personal lives.

'Often enough, we don't even realize who we are meant to be, because we are so busy trying to live out someone else's ideas. Other people do not hold the power to define our destiny. Anyone can be successful if people just would acknowledge their ability to surrender their plans, dreams and goals to a power that is greater than all other people, and greater than themselves. That is the Spirit!'.

www.spiritinfinance.nl

Recommended Reading

INNOVATIVE MINDS

The Economics of Happiness, Mark Anielski
Spirit in Finance (Dutch), Ivo Valkenburg
The Money of the Future , Bernard Lietaer
Of Human Wealth; Beyond Greed and Scarcity, Bernard Lietaer &
    Stefan Brunnhuber
Fooled by Randomness, Nassim Nicholas Taleb
New Green Deal (Dutch), Wouter van Dieren
The Transition Handbook, Rob Hopkins
Hot, flat, & Crowded, Thomas Friedman
Interest and Inflation Free Money, Margrit Kennedy
Regional currencies – new paths towards sustainable growth,
    Margrit Kennedy
Semco Style, Ricardo Semler
The Seven-Day Weekend, Ricardo Semler
Ethical Markets, Hazel Henderson
The New Economy of Nature, Gretchen Daily & Katherine Ellison
Cradle to Cradle: Remaking the Way We Make Things,
    William McDonough & Michael Braungart
The Wisdom of Sustainability, Sulak Sivaraksa
Living the Simple Life, Elaine St.James

INVESTIGATORS AND HISTORIANS

Tragedy & Hope, Carrol Quigley
Wall Street and the Rise of Hitler, Anthony Sutton
Hot, flat and crowded, Thomas Friedman
Beyond the crisis, Adjiedj Bakar
Big Business with Nazi-Germany (Dutch), Jacques R. Pauwels
Consumed, Benjamin R. Barber
The Two Trillion Dollar Meltdown, Charles P. Morris
Confessions of an Economic Hitman, John Perkins
Hoodwinked, John Perkins
The Globalization of Poverty, Michel Chossudovsky
The Global Economic Crisis, Michel Chossudovsky & Andrew
    Marshall (editors)
Terrorism and The Economy, Loretta Napoleoni
Rogue Economics, Loretta Napoleoni
The Great Derangement, Matt Taibi
The History of Money, Jack Weatherford
*A History of Money and Banking in the United States, the Colonial
    Era to World War II*, Murray N. Rothbard
History of Money from Ancient Times to the Present Day,
    Glen Davies
History of Money in the British empire & the United States,
    Agnes F. Dodd
Money as Debt I, 2007, Paul Grignon (available on DVD), and
    Money as Debt II 2010, Paul Grignon (available on DVD)
Der Mythos vom Geld-Die Geschichte der Macht, Stephen Zarlenga
The French Connection, The History of the House of Rothschild,
    Andrew Hitchcock (digital)
End the FED, Ron Paul
The Naked Capitalist, W. Cleon Skousen
The Secrets of the Federal Reserve, Eustace Mullins

ECONOMISTS

Free Fall, Joseph Stiglitz
Globalization and its Discontents, Joseph Stiglitz
A short History of Financial Euphoria, John Kenneth Galbraith
The Affluent Society (revised 2009), John Kenneth Galbraith
The Great Contraction 1929-1933, Milton Friedman and Anna
    Schwartz
Capitalism and freedom, Milton Friedman
The General Theory of Employment, Interest, and Money,
    John M. Keynes & Paul Krugman
Small Is Beautiful, E.F. Schumacher
The Conscience of a liberal, Paul Krugman
What has Government done to our Money, Murray N. Rothbard
The Mystery of Banking, Murray N. Rothbard

INVESTORS AND BUSINESSMEN

Lessons from the Legends of Wall Street, Nikki Ross
The New Paradigm for Financial Markets, George Soros
The Crash of 2008, George Soros
The Road Ahead, Bill Gates

OTHER

OECD Studies on SMEs: Entrepreneurship and Innovation
(15 June 2010), OECD
The Value Profit Chain, James L. Heskett, W. Earl Sasser &
Leonard A. Schlesinger
Activity-Based Costing: Making it Work for SMEs, Douglas T. Hicks
Pocket World in Figures, The Economist

www.ingramcontent.com/pod-product-compliance
Lightning Source LLC
LaVergne TN
LVHW091455170726
843492LV00001B/197